Empty Pages

A Search for Writing Competence in School and Society

Clifton Fadiman and James Howard

Signature Books

Fearon Pitman Publishers, Inc., Belmont, California,
in association with the Council for Basic Education

Editor: Suzanne Lipset
Design and Typography: Polycarp Press
Cover Design: William Nagel Graphic Design

ISBN-0-8224-2701-X (paperbound)

ISBN-0-8224-2700-1 (casebound)

Library of Congress Catalog Card Number: 79-52662

Printed in the United States of America.

1.9 8 7 6 5 4 3 2 1

The writing done or not done today is a result of ideas and attitudes that pervade society. It is not chargeable solely to the school world; it is a cultural and not simply an educational failure.

Jacques Barzun

Contents

Acknowledgments

This book was made possible by a grant to the Council for Basic Education, Washington, D.C., from the National Endowment for the Humanities. With the help of the grant, the council formed the Commission on Writing consisting of

- Clifton Fadiman, Chairman
- Jacques Barzun, Consultant
- James Howard, Project Director
- Mary L. Burkhardt, Director of Reading, Rochester City School District, Rochester, New York
- William W. Cook, Director of English 2, Department of English, Dartmouth College, Hanover, New Hampshire
- Lois DeBakey, Professor of Scientific Communication, Baylor College of Medicine, Houston, Texas
- Joan Butterworth Grady, Administrative Liaison, English Department, Laredo–Cherry Creek Schools, Colorado
- Doris Carson Jackson, Teacher of English, Pelham Memorial High School, Pelham, New York
- Paul Kalkstein, Coordinator of the English Competence Program, Phillips Academy, Andover, Massachusetts
- Charles Scribner, Jr., Chairman of the Board, Charles Scribner's Sons, New York, New York
- Arn Tibbetts, Director of Rhetoric, University of Illinois, Urbana, Illinois

By generously sharing their research papers, knowledge, experience, and counsel, the consultant and the eight commissioners are in large part responsible for this book.

We would also like to acknowledge with gratitude the help of Siu Zimmerman, William Russell, Lucille Murray, Ellen Shepherd, and Joseph Dominic.

Introduction

Empty Pages is about writing as a human act that is both necessary and rewarding. It is not a manual of "correct English," a guide to the perplexed writer, or an indictment of our schools. It stresses teaching and learning in the English class, but views these activities as parts of general education and as affected by social pressures exerted outside the classroom walls—indeed by the whole of our culture. The book does consider the unsatisfactory state of writing currently prevailing in our elementary and secondary schools, and it analyzes the origins of that state, together with possible alternatives open to both teacher and student. We have, however, tried to place our subject in a setting larger than the classroom.

Empty Pages: A Search for Writing Competence in School and Society is based on the work of eleven women and men, including the authors, chosen by the Council for Basic Education to collectively form the Commission on Writing (see page ix). Nine of the commission members are former or practicing educators, whether drawn from elementary and secondary schools or from what the late Robert M. Hutchins, head of the Center for the Study of Democratic Institutions, called (perhaps with a feather-stroke of irony) the Higher Learning in America. The tenth member heads that near relic, a genuine publishing house. The eleventh is a professional writer and editor.

The commissioners do not fly any special educational flag. What binds us is a passion for our magnificent language and a deep concern for the literacy of the American student—and indeed of the American citizen. We also have in common the advantage that we are not "experts" in the field of "compositional theory," but working teachers, writers, and editors.

For more than a year the commission met many times. We exchanged, argued, refuted, and altered views. We submitted papers, each reflecting the special competence of the individual

1

author, and revised them in the light of close discussion and further research. This book is rooted in the papers. Though the text was written by James Howard and me, in some cases certain of the papers seemed to state exactly the next point in our argument or description and were therefore used verbatim or with minor editing.

I have mentioned that our common passion and our common concern were for language and literacy. Back of passion and concern lie certain assumptions animating our every thought. Though we do not hold these truths to be self-evident, we believe that respect for the opinion of the reader requires that we should declare them:

1. The life of any culture rests on that rock-bottom device of social bonding, language.

2. Therefore, the teaching and learning of the language should have as their ultimate goal (in addition to more immediate aims) the continued health and improvement of the culture.

3. One way to achieve this healthy state, as well as to effect the improvement, is to liberate the intelligence of citizens by ensuring that they have the ability to read and write.

4. The liberation of the intelligence should not be confused with "socialization," "acculturation," "self-expression," or the "search for identity." The teaching of language, and notably of writing, should not be subordinated to purely private purposes, let alone fleeting trends or fashions. It should be anchored in the best means of expression so far attained by our culture.

5. English teachers are primarily the best means we have of transmitting language skills. They are not, or should not be, primarily entertainers, welfare workers, group therapists, priest-parson-rabbi surrogates, librarians, or sitters. Even if not primarily so, all teachers (and even administrators) are or should be teachers of English and therefore, to some degree, of writing.

6. The job (insofar as they do not do these things for themselves) is to teach the students to talk, think, read, and write in the language known as Standard English. Oral

Standard English and written Standard English may differ, but the differences between them are less marked than those distinguishing the accepted language from ethnic, dialectical, jargon, or vogue English.

7. Writing is inseparable from thinking, reading, speaking, listening, and studying. Though it has its own norms and uses its own pedagogy, it is part of a circle of connected activities.

8. Since reading and writing are intimately connected, learning to write depends on exposure to high-quality reading material.

9. Teachers themselves must have learned and must continue to practice writing. This obligation rests on them as it does upon the student.

10. Achieving some competence in writing is both the right and the responsibility of all members of a democracy. We cannot afford to reproduce in the domain of literacy the Two Nations—the Poor and the Rich—identified by Disraeli in the domain of property.

11. Clear and effective writing is not simply a skill or a socioeconomic advantage. Because it expresses the integrity (or dishonesty) of an intellectual process, it is a moral activity.

12. Finally, we believe that every normal Jane and Johnny can, if properly taught, learn how to write clearly, competently, and correctly.

We do not expect all twelve of these articles of faith to elicit shouts of unanimous approval. We do, however, respectfully ask that, after reading this book, you reflect upon the validity and importance of these assumptions in the light of that reading.

Defining our audience may help to make our direction clear. Whom are we addressing? First, teachers—not English teachers alone, but all teachers. No teacher exists, basketball coach included, whose daily labors do not involve the ability to use the language and also on occasion to correct it in the speech or writing of students. We are all communicating or being communicated to—incessantly. But, because the teacher's communication directly affects the bent of our children's minds, it is vital. The teacher's influence is more vital than the bureaucrat's or politician's language, which we discount as a dexterous orchestration of banalities; more vital than the broadcaster's language, which increasingly we understand to be a mechanism for lulling, diverting, or bending the intelligence toward a readiness to consume; more vital than the parent's language since the family as a quasi-educational institution has weakened considerably; more vital even than the work of professional writers, for only a minority read it. During our plastic years the teacher is willy-nilly the appointed warden of the language. Others may do their best to guard it, but in any real sense the teacher alone holds the position of prime responsibility.

But this book does not address itself only to the schoolteacher. We hope the academy will read it to good effect as well. Perhaps it will make a little clearer to professors the reasons for their students' inadequacies in composition. Perhaps, by showing them what the schoolteacher must contend with, it will quicken their sympathies, making them more ready to cooperate than to condemn. And if those professors should themselves be teachers of teachers, the book may incline them to take a fresh look at their curricula, syllabi, and methods. It may even induce them to cast a critical eye on their own written and oral language.

We speak also to future teachers, those now preparing for their calling. We earnestly ask them to reflect on some of the issues we raise, such as the quantity of actual *writing* required in the average teacher-training institution and the tendency of so much of that writing to be not Standard English but professional jargon.

We speak finally to the growing number of worried Americans affected by the state of writing in our country: parents surprised at their children's inability to write a letter; government servants aware that the phrasing of their communications produces no real consequences in action; people of affairs who cannot understand their employees' memoranda; professionals and technicians who use a language so special that they can no longer communicate with the rest of us; and responsible school administrators disturbed by the growing evidence of their institutions' incapacity to raise or even flatten the downward curve of literacy. Finally, in the hope that this book may further encourage them, we address ourselves to those scholars now trying to explore the psychological basis of the act of writing.

We've defined our audience, now an introductory word on our approach. Much has been written about the "writing crisis," rather less about writing. No one familiar with the national temperament would find this emphasis surprising. Figures excite us more strongly than ideas, and so we detect a crisis behind every bristle of sad statistics and droopy curves. Moreover, the crisis is presentable as a "problem," which to our technological minds implies a "solution"—always a cheering thought. Then again, we are a pendulum people; we find it easy to swing from the anything-goes educational atmosphere of the sixties and early seventies back to a simple-minded sentimentality about the little red schoolhouse, the spelling bee, and correct punctuation. Finally, the media must live, and crises are their daily food.

The branch of campanology known as alarm-bell ringing may safely be surrendered to the media. This does not imply that the commissioners judge our trouble to be a simple nuisance, manageable, like the traffic law violator, by more stringent laws. On the contrary, we are persuaded that much truth lies in the epigraph to this book, which bears repeating in this context: "The writing done or not done today is a result of ideas and attitudes that pervade society. It is not chargeable solely to the school world; it is a cultural and not simply an educational failure."[1]* The situation involves the whole culture, rather than a self-contained fraction of it.

There is hope: ideas and attitudes are amenable to change, and some evidence exists that they are changing under our very eyes. Citizens in general are yielding their somewhat unfocused indignation, with all its mixed emotions, to the more definite suspicion that while a "well adjusted" child is pleasant to contemplate, a literate one is to be preferred.

Arn Tibbetts, one of our commissioners, writes, "The better schools have one thing in common: a community determined to educate its children."[2] That determination is spreading. Certainly the educational community is beginning to take more interest in examining the "crisis" constructively than in reinforcing fixed positions in a controversy.

Given these changes in attitude, we are encouraged to feel that

*Superscript numerals refer to source notes at the end of this book. Substantive footnotes are indicated by asterisks.

this book is happily timed. Whatever life it has will be lived within an atmosphere at once more truly serious and more truly hopeful than has obtained in the recent past.

Our claims are limited. We have expounded no profound or original doctrine of composition—though it may well be that the times are calling for one. Some readers may encounter unfamiliar insights and counsels, but that is not to call them new, even if a number of them may be so venerable as to appear so. Our hope is that they are true.

The villain? "No villain need be! . . . We are betrayed by what is false within." If, as Mr. Barzun says, the failure is cultural, it has behooved the commissioners to place the seemingly discrete subject of composition within the broadest possible context. Both effective and defective writing come out of a self subtly linked to the whole human environment, past and present. The child who scrawls his first complete sentence—*I see the cat*—is really telling us that he has just seen the world and victoriously fixed it with magic pencil and paper. The writing of that sentence is a social act. In trying to understand why such social acts are being more and more feebly performed, a search for one or more villains will avail us little.

This outlook dictates the form of our argument. We first chart the predicament in which we find our language and weigh the evidence for the decline of writing. (We include some contrary opinions.) Next we list the influences that imperil the well-being of writing even as it is being practiced now. It then seems to us necessary—how peculiar to our era is this necessity—actually to present the cases for and against knowing how to write. But to write what and to write how? Those are the questions next addressed. The prickly issues presented by grammar and the mechanics of writing are also discussed. Then follow two chapters on the conditions of learning and the conditions of teaching. In conclusion we repeat Tolstoy's trenchant question, "What then must we do?" In answering that question we point to a number of promising new alternatives already available to us, whether we are teachers, parents, or, most important of all, children. Finally, the appendices offer some supplementary material of particular and concrete interest to the teaching profession.

A word about the larger context of our subject: This book is by and for Americans about writing in American English. Neither the competence nor the mandate of the commission permits it to seek the consolation that comes of knowing that others are in the same leaky boat. Still, in order to enlarge our vision, it is well to be aware that such troubles as we suffer are not confined to our own soil. Knowing this, we may infer that these troubles cannot be exorcised solely by institutional changes, useful as they may be.

Our Canadian neighbors, though rather more calmly, seem also to be viewing the state of writing with distress. And reports from France, that traditional center of Cartesian clarity, point to a continuing atrophy of the rigorous *lycée* system and to a weakening of the appetite for literacy. Lower schools in France are giving up *dictée* (the taking down and careful study of a dictated model passage), without which French *cannot* be learned correctly or even rightly understood, so frequently does homonymy occur in that language. All the environmental pressures recognizable in the United States are also experienced in France.

In Britain students seem to be in worse straits than in the U.S. The so-called informal methods of teaching used in Britain, though stoutly defended by the "progressives" and part of the educational establishment, do not appear to be working. In a typical London school (St. John's Comprehensive) it was reported, on October 20, 1976, that children of average ability aged fourteen through sixteen were still making the most elementary errors on composition. On October 25 of the same year, an experienced A-level examiner made the point forcibly: "What alarms me more is that few even of the ablest candidates can express themselves as clearly and accurately as the average run of candidates could do 17 years ago." Note that in England records of examination questions and the answers to them—and therefore test scores—have been kept since the late 1890s. Therefore, an exact comparison is possible, and we learn that entrants to teachers' colleges today perform at levels two or three grades below those of 1920.

Consider this story: A devoted Manchester schoolteacher succeeded in teaching all her six-year-olds to begin reading. She was then chided by an adviser-inspector: "All your children can read. You have obviously spent far too much time on the teaching of reading." Does this anecdote help to explain Britain's troubles? Are they explained further by the elaborately "progressive"

Plowden report, which states that the "distinction between work and play is false, possibly throughout life, certainly in primary school"?[3] (Good news for British coal miners.)

I do not adduce these bits and pieces as hard evidence of a parallel decline of writing in other countries. But the chorus of complaints outside our own land is audible enough to force reflection on our subject's size and shape. The more we think about it, the more elusive our subject seems. Is it possible that we are dealing with something beyond even Mr. Barzun's "cultural failure," which presumably he restricts to the United States? Is it possible that, at least in the industrialized free world, seismic forces are at work warning us of some crucial change in the very nature of *homo sapiens* as a cultural animal? Most historians smile gently at such airy speculations. But others suggest that an emergent world-wide technoculture is announcing itself by, among other signals, a shift away from traditional literacy, a shift more far-reaching in its effect than the one from manuscript to printed book.

A technoculture would actively *sustain* illiterates, rather than, as now, passively tolerating them. Have we not seen in the recent past considerable support for the idea of such sustenance? Some educators, and not frivolously, have posed the question, Is an education itself necessarily a high priority in the student's mind? Proposals for deschooling society may seem less wild if seen as a kind of heralding of the future.

We on the commission are not instant sociologists or philosophers of history. Nor are we attracted to doom-and-gloom theories, however modish they may be. We do not avoid the grim issue the doom-and-gloom theories present, but we are by nature averse to giving it a central place in the discussion. We have other fish to fry, smaller fish perhaps, but our own.

And yet, before readers plunge into our subject, it may be salutary for them to stop and wonder, as we have, what that subject ultimately includes. Is the concern only with the teaching of composition in the schools? Or are we facing some premonitory evidence of a shattering evolutionary change in human history?

We have written this book in the belief that our field is limited and manageable, that it can yield conclusions that will be immediately useful—conclusions we earnestly hope may be heeded, revised if need be, and then acted upon.

Clifton Fadiman

Chapter 1

A Time of Trouble

Seniors who were to be graduated from a New York City high school in 1978 wrote the lines displayed below. They were taken at random from homework papers selected by the students' English teacher, a seventeen-year veteran of the school system, and printed in the *New York Times*.[1] The essays, she said, were typical of most student writing and should be published to show why so many teachers have become discouraged.

One student, writing of Anne Frank, began her essay this way:

> This is a idea of a tragedy the reason is that Anne Frank lived through a very hard live. Her family and Anne are German and Hitler doesn't like germans, so Hitler passed a law for germans to be captured and put to work and maybe even killed.

Another student read the book *Dibs in Search of Self* and began her essay this way:

> This is my idea of a Trageic life Dibs a five year old boy, he wasn't understood by his parent's the first year of his life was very sad he din't have any friends, he din't speak at all, in the classrooms he sat by himself.

Having thus supplied living examples of the trouble we face as a literate society, let us attempt to assess the problem's dimensions. As noted in the introduction, *crisis* is the electronic media's word: we face neither a writing crisis nor a reading crisis. We are not about to become a nation of total illiterates. Nor on the other hand will any nostrum magically cure us. The patient will neither expire nor spring from bed like a son of the morning.

But there *is* a bed and in it lies a patient. Let the cloudy term *trouble* describe the illness. We are all in some sort of trouble, most thoughtful readers agree, over the teaching and learning of writing. What sort of trouble? How much trouble? What kinds of teaching and learning? What kinds of writing? Who is ailing? Should the patient be helped? Or should we merely remain observant, diagnosing the condition as a normal part of the birth trauma accompanying the appearance of a new type of human being—a nonliterate citizen in a fully technological culture? But if the patient should and can be helped, who should go about it? To such matters this book addresses itself.

Impressions of the Problem

An encouraging word: we have made some progress since the unshackled sixties. In that turbulent decade a college dean whom we won't identify could define an educated man as "one who is well-adjusted and helpful in his community." This same dean answered "yea" when asked if such a one could be judged educated even if he couldn't count his fingers or write his name. But let us not be too pleased with ourselves. A number of commentators claim that the number of functional illiterates in the nation as a whole approximates 23 million.* In the mid-seventies Norvell Northcutt, head of the Adult Performance Level Project, reported to the U.S. Office of Education that one-fifth of the adults in the United States get along poorly because of deficient communication skills, especially reading and writing. But the definiteness of statistics is a little like the demeanor of the man

---

*In "Back to Basics in the Schools," George Weber defines *functional illiterate* this way: "An adult or young person who lacks the reading and writing ability to cope with the minimal economic, social, cultural, and political demands of daily living in today's society. Sometimes extended to include arithmetic and rudimentary practical knowledge. Modern society takes for granted a relatively high level of literacy. The result is a paradox: because of the achievement of ever higher levels of education, modern America has become so literate that it has far more 'functional illiterates' (both in numbers and as a percentage of the population) than was the case a century ago. Exactly what the present minimal functional literacy level is, is open to debate, but it certainly includes the ability to read and write well enough to get and to perform satisfactorily the most routine jobs; to fill out common forms; to read an average daily newspaper, signs, instructions, and directions; and to write simple messages and letters. Roughly 15 percent of American young people are functional illiterates." From George Weber, "Back to Basics in the Schools" (unpublished manuscript, pp. 187–88).

who always looks you straight in the eye. There's something suspicious about it. The nonquantifiable may be more persuasive. When we hear that corporations are deserting New York because, among the many other reasons that city so efficiently provides, they can't find clerical workers with minimum literacy skills, we begin to wonder. *Newsweek* quotes a personnel officer at the Bank of America: ". . . errors we once found commonly in applications from the high-school graduates are now cropping up in forms from people with four-year college degrees."[2]

A situation that arose in 1977 in Burlington, Vermont, is typical of the business community's growing dissatisfaction. Industrial leaders found that young job-hunters had trouble merely filling out application forms. Four of the district's major industrial concerns—Digital Equipment Corporation, General Electric, Simmonds Precision, and Hayward Tyler Pump—formed a committee to pressure Vermont educators. Peter Bowen, organizer of this group, believes the trouble lies in the drift away from basic education. "Too much freedom," says Bowen.[3]

An editorial in the September 1977 issue of *Administrative Management* clearly expresses what many members of the managerial class across the country are now thinking:

> Communication is at the core of executive performance. It's what office work is all about. The cloudy instruction, the poorly organized memo impede understanding like so much static on the radio. Ungrammatical and misspelled correspondence reflects badly upon the sender and his firm. They all invite waste, confusion, and annoyance.

Let us put in strong terms the relation between the private enterprise system and literacy. When all is said and done, most high school graduates are going into industry. Our trouble is not that we are not developing good writers. It is that we are not educating people so they can write well enough to keep a job. Is it too much to say that the continued existence of the system on which all of us depend is tied to a general ability to read and write? If we are to listen to industry itself, we get that impression.

On February 22, 1976, Robert H. McBride, past president of the National Association of State Boards of Education, made an extraordinary report at the annual meeting of the American Association of School Administrators.[4] McBride decided to get the facts about the business world's satisfaction with the competences of young people by interviewing personnel people in five large businesses, three of them with annual sales over $1 billion. We offer a brief summary of the main conclusions.

- Company A: "Basic deficiencies in graduates were inability to spell . . . and to write or speak Standard English."
- Company B: "Inability to either write or to organize coherently a set of facts is a major problem. Overall, thinks that student performance and achievement is worse than related by the press."
- Company C: "The high school diploma is valueless. . . . Things are actually worse than portrayed in the press."
- Company D: "Graduates are not getting the basics in math and English."
- Company E: "An overriding problem in graduates is inability to communicate—both verbally and in writing reports. . . . Incidentally, noted that inability to write was becoming more and more a problem even with college graduates."

With respect to this latter point, Company A reported that one college graduate "couldn't hold down a messenger job in the summer and another had difficulty in finding his way in a records center." The reader might be anxious about the fate of these two unfortunate youths. They are both now substitute teachers in a city school.

The business world's melancholy is shared by the military, the realm of technology, and especially the government bureaucracy, which has itself contributed so energetically to the degeneration of the language. The Civil Service Commission, for example, was recently forced to double its in-house remedial writing programs.

Perhaps we adults can roughly measure our literacy by using as a standard that large class of people whose very trade requires clear and correct language: newspaper journalists. On November

1, 1977, columnist James J. Kilpatrick reported that a group of Associated Press managing editors was viewing young journalists' copy with a jaundiced eye. "Their sentences wander off in all directions," wrote Kilpatrick, "their spelling is only so-so; their sense of organization is seldom very keen. . . . The most common fault is the imprecise word."[5] If people whose job is to write can't write, what about the rest of us? Are we not quicker to behold the mote of illiteracy in our children's eye than to consider the beam in our own?

The Testimony of the Tests

We use the word testimony in the heading of this section. But perhaps we cannot call the available test data evidence; assuredly they do not represent hardcore proof. In estimating the dimensions of the trouble we at once bump up against a discomfiting fact. English, including English composition, isn't really a discrete subject, a solid body of facts, laws, or conclusions transmittable as a unit. It is teachable—but we are not sure what the "it" is. Whether we are measuring competence in literature or composition, there is something chancy about trying to measure with quantitative test-scoring techniques either absolute proficiency or relative progress. The modern technology of assessment must contend with some difficulties. The facts are that the writing skills of large groups are rarely tested validly over a significant time period, that when tests are administered factors are omitted or are difficult to measure, that test responses are often open to subjective interpretation by the scorers, and that frequently in test situations a control group is altogether absent. At times "English" seems elusive, like a gas. Hence, grading a composition, like grading a human being, sometimes involves a high degree of uncertainty.

Mindful of such caveats, we still cannot dismiss out of hand the testimony that ignited the media's dry tinder. So that all readers may have the same general picture in mind, it is portrayed briefly below.

The National Assessment of Educational Progress (NAEP) is a federally funded program conducted by the Education Commission of the States. It uses the techniques of standardized testing and national polling to survey the achievement of the nation's students in art, career and occupational development, citizenship, and the basic academic subjects taught in school. NAEP made its first appraisal of writing ability during 1969–1970.[6] It tested nine-year-olds, thirteen-year-olds, seventeen-year-olds, and young adults (aged twenty-six through thirty-five) with survey questions, multiple-choice questions, and an essay requirement.* The essays were judged on mechanical correctness and rhetorical competence; they were also considered "holistically" (academese for general impression). The tests were repeated in 1974. Assessments of the results and the "decline" noted over the four-to-five year period between tests are responsible for much of the media's agitation and the public's response to it.

Here are a few of the findings, stated in summary form by the assessors. The causes of these results—ethnic, social, economic—are far less clear than the results themselves. And neither we nor the NAEP will make extravagant claims for their statistical basis.

• Nine-year-olds: Little change in the average quality of the essay, perhaps even some indication of a modest increase in achievement through grade 4, but a widening gap between the good compositions and the poor ones.

• Thirteen-year-olds: Overall decline in the essays, with the proportion of "very good writers" dropping from 19 percent to 13 percent.

• Seventeen-year-olds: Overall decline in the essays, though no evidence of decline in mechanics. The poor writers get worse and proportionately more numerous. Essays show a general movement toward the conventions of spoken English and away from those of written English.

In commenting on the meaning of these findings, Richard Lloyd-Jones, former chair of the Conference on College Com-

---

*The essay component should be considered in light of the average student's notion of what constitutes a "composition." In 1974, when the tests were repeated, the average seventeen-year-old student produced a paper 137 words long, composed of sentences averaging 16 words. This is less than a normal page of normal handwriting. It represents *all* the student could think of when faced with a given topic—though, of course, working within a time limit.

position and Communication, and Ross Winterowd, former chair of the NCTE Commission on Composition, are sanguine enough to say that "what appears 'incoherent' to us today will some day be very easy to understand." However, they are reluctant to use such grounds to excuse the student. While Lloyd-Jones at one point is skeptical about the significance of the test results, he and Winterowd at another point agree in calling the general trend "disturbing." Significantly, they are most disturbed by the growing "polarization of good and bad writers." This phenomenon is probably more important than any given set of statistics.

Roy H. Forbes, director of NAEP, flatly concludes, "The written word is in trouble and demands immediate attention."[7] And, commenting on the 1969 survey (mechanics only), the Council for Basic Education notes, "The poorest 17-year-olds did a little worse than the average 9-year-olds." With respect to the 1974 survey, the Council admits mournfully, "Unfortunately, the results, over all, are even worse."[8]

Our personal conclusion, keeping in mind various cautions (such as the absence of a "complete" set of controls and the contention of some that the "crisis" simply may reflect our new methods for studying these matters), is that, whether over a five-year period the curve has risen, fallen, or remained flat, the national level of writing competence is unacceptably low.

At this point we feel obliged to make some statement about the decline in Scholastic Aptitude Test scores, although it will become clear that we do not feel that either this test or the history of students' scores on it has much to do with writing competence. It is common knowledge that from 1964 to 1977 scores on the verbal section of the SAT declined in every year but one. The educational community was so alarmed that a national panel of twenty-one distinguished persons, headed by former Secretary of Labor Willard Wirtz, was named to study the decline. After two years of deliberation, the panel issued its report, "On Further Examination."[9] The report attributes the pre-1970 decline partly to mass changes in the makeup of the college-bound population. "Erosion of academic standards in high school" is cited as one major reason for the post-1970 decline. Of particular interest is that the panel saw a connection between the general decline and the diminishing amount of "critical reading and careful writing" and suggested that these two traditional academic activities be restored to a primary place in the curriculum. (The panel also opined that "secondary education must become still more diversified, more varied—but without being watered down." A nice trick, we judge, if you can do it.)

But at least in the context of our concerns, neither the SAT nor the decline in scores may add up to much. The Council for Basic Education considers the score decline "interesting" (a word, one imagines, they may have substituted for "suspicious"), but doubts that the SAT is a very good measure of overall academic achievement, although it may be useful in the college admission process.[10] Many well-informed observers (including some most concerned about the decline in writing) do not consider the verbal part of the SAT a valid indicator of writing ability, since it is a multiple-choice test requiring no actual composition. It can and has been handled brilliantly by students who cannot write very well. Evidence: In the fall of 1975 Stanford's entering freshman class contained a goodly number of students who had scored over 700 on the SAT English Achievement Test (more demanding than the more general SAT verbal aptitude section), but three-fourths of that high-scoring group failed the university's own English placement test, which emphasizes *writing*.

Our conclusion is that the argument over the SAT bears little relationship to our concern for writing competence. If it signifies anything, that significance is miniscule compared to the gross fact that 15 percent of our young people are functionally illiterate, and many of the rest disappoint those who eventually employ them. Finally, our concern in this book is with all young Americans, whether or not college bound. In this regard, consider how Raymond English, director of the social studies program of the Educational Research Council of America, described a September 1976 conference on education and citizenship:

> One of the speakers at the citizenship conference, Abigail Van Buren, provided first-hand evidence of our deteriorating education. Out of the average ten thousand letters she receives each week those written by persons under thirty are regularly far more inarticulate, illiterate, and ungrammatical than those from the older generation. That, Dear Abby, seems more cogent than declining SAT scores.[11]

Still, test data do prove that a problem exists, and the nation-wide tests, whatever importance is attached to them, may be said to confirm on a large scale the results of tests carried out locally. An instance from California may be characteristic. In early January 1977, as part of a minimum competence project, a task force of teachers in San Bernardino's El Cajon high school gave the school's 1,376 students an essay-writing test. They found that a full 60 percent "couldn't write a simple sentence . . . couldn't maintain and develop an idea." Over half of the remaining 40 percent had difficulty separating their sentences into paragraphs and organizing their thoughts, and were judged not to have the minimum skills necessary to write at the high school level. Joann Mercer, English department chairman who headed the task force, suggested that one reason the students wrote so badly was that they didn't read much. "They have so little experience with reading they don't know how the language sounds," she said.[12]

It is bad enough that in a Honolulu school not one ninth-grader could write the Pledge of Allegiance correctly, or that twelve misspelled America. But when we hear of hundreds of such small horrors, emanating from every state in the union, we begin to understand why—test scores or no test scores, media alarmism or no media alarmism—large numbers of citizens are becoming militant over the issue. They may not have studied the complex problem thoroughly, but their frustration and ire match perfectly the quiet conclusion reached by the Sloan Foundation after interviewing many authorities: "These persons have reinforced the Foundation's belief that American students, whether better or worse at expository writing, are unacceptably deficient now."[13]

And the ultimate voice, that of the federal bureaucracy, speaks in the person of Joseph Califano, secretary of Health, Education and Welfare: "The American people—in return for the millions of tax dollars they spend on education—are demanding that a basic level of competence, a set of minimum skills, be transmitted by our elementary and secondary schools to their students."

Alarm in the Colleges

In the past, the college was not duty-bound to teach mere writing *competence*. The present valiant efforts of colleges to teach their students how to write reflect an exceptional condition. Still, more than a generation ago, in 1950 (when the villain television was only a nine-year-old urchin), John M. Stalnaker, later to serve as president of the National Merit Scholarship Corporation, reported, "College teachers are finding that more and more freshmen, even those with high aptitude test scores and brilliant school records, are unable to express themselves with reasonable accuracy and clarity." And eleven years later George B. Leonard stated, "Writing is the disgrace of American education."[14]

Today such intermittent reports have multiplied. If only a few colleges were complaining about the writing capacities of entering freshmen, or if only high-standard Ivy League colleges were complaining, such testimony might be questioned. Taken as a whole, however, the reports are troubling.

The state of California offers telling examples. One case involves the writing skills of incoming freshmen in the state's prestigious university system. In November 1976, a report to the Regents' Educational Policy Committee noted that an increasing number of students were not achieving the university's standards on the College Board's English Composition Test, required of all applicants for admission. The ECT is a multiple-choice test requiring no actual writing, but measuring correctness and effectiveness of language, organizational sensitivity, and sensitivity to appropriate language; a score of 600 or better is a "pass" as far as the University of California is concerned. Between 1968 and 1975, the number of freshmen system-wide who made that score dropped from an already alarming 32 percent to 25 percent. (Over the same period, UCLA's pass rate dropped from 31 percent to 21 percent.) The remaining three-fourths of those freshmen in 1975 then had to take the university's own Subject A essay test. Failure on this test relegates one to the labors of the Subject A course, better known in peer circles as "bonehead English." In 1975, as in other recent years, about 50 percent of those taking the essay test failed it, but 90 percent of those taking the course succeeded on the exam when it was given again as a course final. This result indicates (the report notes) that "for the majority of students, the problem lies not in a lack of natural ability or intelligence, but simply in the nature of previous instruction."[15]

We consider it noteworthy that the lack in "previous instruction," which presumably deepens through several years of a student's schooling, is a deficiency the university can remedy for most students in five months of instruction. Note also that although not all students coming to the University of California are prepared by California high schools, those from within the state are from the top 12 percent of their graduating classes, and those from without are at least as select a group. When, as in 1975–1976, almost half of a student group of this caliber had to take bonehead, there is at least cause for concern.

At Stanford University, a similar situation pertains. As of 1976, three-fourths of the freshmen who scored 700 or higher (top scoring) on the College Board English achievement test (it was multiple choice) nonetheless had to study remedial composition because they failed the university's own writing test, similar to the University of California's Subject A exam.

Asked whether student skills are declining, Professor Edward M. White of California State College at San Bernardino answered that he did think such a decline had taken place. And this subjective opinion is buttressed by the telling observation that White's own composition textbooks, intended for freshmen, are now often used in advanced composition courses.

We have cited California testimony rather fully. In the past certain states or regions, not unlike certain individual heroes, have at various times served as national models: Virginia, Massachusetts, New York City. That position, we think, is now, and for the immediate future will be, occupied by California. With respect to the national feeling for general ideals of culture and style, as California goes so goes the nation.

Furthermore, the inadequacies of California's students occur in spite of the fact that the per capita expenditure on education in that state is the highest in the country. Apparently a generous budget does not guarantee literacy.

However, the problem is hardly limited to California campuses. Elissa S. Guralnik and Paul M. Levitt, both of the University of Colorado, described the situation there: "The quality of student writing had declined so precipitously that faculty from all departments and schools were complaining." These teachers complain of "no knowledge of grammar" and, more to the point, of the fact that some students "had written no more than three papers in three years of high school."[16] The University of Colorado determined to do something, and beginning in the fall of

1977 all freshmen at the College of Arts and Sciences were required to write an essay to be evaluated by the English Department, the unsuccessful to attend remedial English.

Example follows example, from all parts of the country, all levels of academic excellence:

• At the Urbana-Champaign campus of the University of Illinois, the mean student score on the rhetoric proficiency and placement test given to incoming freshmen fell from 529 in 1968 to 470 in 1974. The fall has continued without interruption since 1970. The 5 percent decline between 1972 and 1975 corresponds to the national SAT decline.

• In its issue of December 8, 1975, *Newsweek* reported that the proportion of freshmen failing an English placement examination (character not indicated) given at Temple University, in Philadelphia, had increased by more than 50 percent since 1968.

• In the fall of 1975, about 11 percent of freshmen at Michigan State University had to take the remedial course. An English instructor there reported that even though students could converse as sophisticated, aware eighteen-year-olds, they wrote like ten-year-olds.

• In 1976 Yale instituted remedial English for the first time since the late 1950s. The course was designed for the one hundred or so students admitted each year who are simply incapable of writing at the college level.

• L. Pearce Williams, who teaches the history of science at Cornell, stated, "Freshman are illiterate on the third-grade level instead of on the eighth-grade level."[17] The university has since launched "a war on illiteracy," proposing to spend $1 million a year waging it.

• Telling evidence (though only of reading ability) that applies to college students across the nation is a pamphlet issued by the Association of American Publishers intended to help college students *read their own textbooks*. To do this it was necessary to use ninth-grade language in the pamphlet rather than the twelfth-grade level used in the textbooks. A report that the association is at work on a second pamphlet to help students read the first pamphlet is pure canard.

The foregoing instances could be multiplied. But they suffice to show that the colleges are up against something they should not be required to handle, something with roots reaching far back into the undergraduate's earlier life.

The Nonalarmist View

Not everyone in the nation, however, is in agreement as to the meaning of the testimony of the tests and the complaints from the colleges. Those who prefer to view the situation without alarm fall into three classes: those who see conditions as no different than in the past, those who are simply unpersuaded by the evidence, and those who ask flatly, Why write? The last group, loosely termed the McLuhanites, will be discussed in detail in Chapter 3. The views of the first two are covered in this chapter.

Those who see the present as a mere continuation of the past view the situation more in sorrow than in anger. While recognizing the inadequacy of student writing, this group deems writing no worse now than it ever was. Says Donald C. Stewart, associate professor of English, Kansas State University, "The discovery that many college-bound students are poor writers is hardly new, except to the most recent discoverers of the fact."[18] Some qualified observers are even more cheerful. The New York Times quotes Malcolm Laws, professor of English, University of Pennsylvania: "While the freshmen on the whole are far from perfect, I don't think they're quite as bad as the groups of freshmen we used to get twenty years ago."[19]

Another nonalarmist is Gary Tate of Texas Christian. He is quoted in Joan Baum's "The Politics of Back-to-Basics": "I have observed no significant decline in writing ability in my 18 years of teaching freshmen." However, Baum comments, "He means: Surface errors have always been around and they are no better or worse, but there is a decline of something."[20]

For some mysterious reason Dartmouth appears to have remained an oasis of (comparative) literacy. "There has been no decline in literacy among Dartmouth students in the 11 years I've been here," says David J. Bradley. "I've been teaching for 15 years—here and at Harvard—and I don't think there's any new crisis in writing," agrees Charles Wood, chairman of the history department. On undergraduate writing in general, however, Dr. Wood comments, ". . . [it] has no character at all."

Whether or not there has been a decline, Dartmouth has decided to play it safe by instituting a new writing clinic. Its founder, Peter Bien, making no comparisons with the immediate past, prefers to sum up the trouble this way: "Very few of our freshmen can write their own language without serious errors (not to mention confused thought). . . . Note that I speak not only for our so-called disadvantaged students, but of all undergraduates." He refers to them as "verbal cripples." Karen Pelz, professor of English, believes the difficulty can be summed up in one word: underexposure.[21]

The second group of the less agitated comprises those not persuaded by the testimony of the tests. Rexford Brown, of the National Assessment of Educational Progress feels "that the [NAEP] evidence, examined closely, is skimpy." Yet he finds himself "willing to *assume* there is a crisis on such little evidence." Richard Lloyd-Jones, quoted earlier, feels that the ACT and SAT tests "are not directly related to writing ability"; and, while conceding that the scores on the writing portions of the NAEP are more significant, reminds us that "NAEP testers have not yet solved the problem of getting written discourse that has been revised beyond a first draft on topics of real interest to the writer."[22]

Those skeptical of the test evidence also often point out that statistical conclusions, drawn from a mass of data that are often ambiguous and rarely buttressed by adequate controls, are only moderately reliable. Among the unpersuaded are those who stress the enormous difference between the roughly homogeneous, college-bound body of thirty years ago and the mixed-up, multileveled mass of college-bound today.

In general, these demurrers are probably rooted in that uneasy feeling, noted above, that the entire discipline once called *English* tends to elude quantitative testing. Yet it remains true of these two groups of nonalarmists that, though they assess the situation differently from the alarmists, they too feel, to use Joan Baum's properly fuzzy phrase, that "there is a decline of something." And most of the nonalarmists feel they should do something about this something.

Chapter 2

Writing and the Environment

We have tried to appraise the rough dimensions of the problem of inadequate writing skills among students of all ages. But to sense the shifting shape of the problem, detect its under- and over- tones, and distinguish shades and variations, we must examine the soil that nourishes it, the cultural and social environment wherein it thrives. This chapter therefore deals not so much with "causes" (the word claims too much) as with those environmental pressures that seem to enfeeble the students' will and reduce their ability to write.

These pressures have been listed by many observers. Yet it is useful to rehearse them once more, not to swell the chorus of woe, but to stimulate us to note how many factors are at work and how densely they pervade our national life. These pressures seem to appear at all points and in all sectors of society; such a total infiltration suggests less a neatly patchable rip than some widespread damage affecting the entire social fabric.

How shall we categorize these pressures? To do so is at best an unsatisfactory business. They overlap or conflict, we do not really know how to weight them, and all tabulations are incomplete. We shall do our best to locate the roots of the problem in five areas: the family and community, the peer group, the media, the available models, and the culture in general. Chapters 5 and 6 survey the more restricted environment shared by student and teacher.

The Family and the Community

What has the family to do with the covering of clean paper with correct squiggles? After all, schools were invented not because the home had failed to advance the child's literacy but because the school was a more efficient agent. Essentially the home is not tutorial, nor should it be. Mothers and fathers teach living, not reading and writing.

Yet since Gutenberg the case has not been quite so simple. Reading and writing have evolved from rarely encountered special talents into skills imbedded in our routine conduct. In somewhat the same way, watching television has changed during the last few decades from a diversion into an indissoluble feature of life itself. Indeed, we have become so habituated to literacy that perhaps we can imagine what its loss would mean to us only by imagining the sudden elimination of television.

It is in the home that the organic connection between life and literacy is first made. If not made there, it may never be made at all or only with difficulty. Parents and older siblings furnish our first and really only important early models of talking, listening, reading, and writing. The happy influence of language should be felt soon. That is why in the modern home the disappearance of the old oaken bookshelf that hung on the wall is a serious matter. So is the disappearance of dinner-table chatter and the bedtime story. Words come 'to mean something to us (educationese: become internalized) when they are associated with the voice boxes of our own family and so, by imitation, with our own vocal cords. They mean less when they pass through a mechanical membrane such as the telephone, the radio tube, or the television screen. Why is it that many of us speak (not to say read or write) worse than our grandparents even though the media of communication have multiplied? We *connect* with the sound of the mother's voice, and so learn from it. To connect with a television character is a different matter entirely. E. B. White, in one of his rare bleak moments, writes, "Short of throwing away all the television sets, I really don't know what we can do about writing."

There still exist millions of American homes where true connection is constantly being made. But in tens of millions connection is fading. Lois DeBakey, professor of scientific communication at Baylor College of Medicine in Houston and a member of our commission, takes a critical view:

Families play musical homes today, moving frequently from one house to another across town or across country. Children may travel miles to go to school, and their parents may do the same to go to work. The steady disintegration of the

family since the eighteenth century, when it was a self-suffi-
cient unit, has curtailed family companionship, conversation—and influence. The earlier agrarian (producer) family,
including the children, not only worked together but played
together, whereas children of the post-industrial (consumer)
family are isolated physically and psychologically from the
world of their parents. Increasingly since World War II,
mothers, traditionally the prime socializing force for children, have been emerging from the home to enter the labor
ranks. The availability of domestic labor-saving devices and
the women's liberation movement have accelerated this
trend, and coincidentally, have diminished the socializing
influence of the mother on the child. Nurses, baby sitters,
and child-care centers have become maternal surrogates, but
do not always provide the verbal and educational stimuli
children need.

Even when both parents are intact in the home (in less
than half the families of elementary schoolchildren),
parents and children may have little in common to talk
about. The architecture of modern homes, which often
segregates children's bedrooms in a special wing, further discourages family camaraderie. Increasingly, moreover, children return home from school to an empty house, which
evokes a sense of loneliness and desolation. . . . Many
parents unwind from the day's pressures by escaping into the
mindless world of television, which requires no conversation
and little concentration. The affluent consumer-parent, accustomed to "buying" whatever he needs, is likely to hire a
tutor for his children rather than assist, himself, with their
lessons. On weekends, parents usually pursue their own
diversionary activities—often at some distance from home,
but rarely with their children. Commercialized entertainment has, unfortunately, almost totally eliminated family
recreation.

Children, thus left to their own devices for companionship, will usually turn to their peers—and largely unsuper-
vised affairs—or will be lured into undesirable activities by
exploitative adults. The resulting schism between children
and parents intensifies the adolescent's sense of alienation

from the seemingly callous world of adults, complicates his eventual assimilation into society, and accentuates his rebelliousness. Such rebelliousness is liable to manifest itself in school, where neglected children may be more interested in retaliation than in writing.[1]

There are, of course, many middle-class and lower-class homes where solidarity and comradeship not only persist, but where, just because these virtues are threatened, extra effort is devoted to cultivating them. Yet the picture Dr. DeBakey draws does apply to many families, and its connection with general literacy cannot be denied.

We said that the home is not directly tutorial. But certain domestic codes of courtesy, now discouraged by the triumph of indulgence, can be indirectly tutorial. The thank-you note, about which children have never been enthusiastic, nonetheless once forced them to associate a natural feeling, that of gratitude, with the activity of writing. Letter-writing in general used to be part of the home's courtesy code. Though the monthly bills in households with teenagers hardly confirm the claim, the telephone is reputed to save time. But that it also saves children from the practice of writing is undeniable. Keeping a diary, formerly a lively and subtle instructive home activity, is now, in modern parlance, a drag, bad news, except among a minority.

To indict the home as the seminary of illiteracy would be unbalanced. But when the Wirtz report, not given to sweeping judgments, cites the increase (at the rate of three hundred thousand per year) of children from homes with fewer (the report prefers "less") than two parents, it is hard not to accept the report's conjecture that such changes have a negative effect on students' entrance examination scores.*

Along with the weakening of the home as an incubator of early literacy goes the weakening of the community. Neighborhood play, a splendid spur to language use, begins to disappear. The Sunday School once helped to furnish models of speaking and writing. Does it still do so? Children rarely visit each other; they visit each other's electronic exhibits. And so we could pile up the

---

*In Chapter 5, some alternatives for changing the negative effects into positive ones are discussed.

evidence that the neighborhood, as a specific institution, is losing its vigor as an informal center of talk. No one argues for a return to the simplicities of Mark Twain's Hannibal, Missouri. But their disappearance may stimulate us to invent some helpful replacements.

The Peer Group

David Riesman, in *The Lonely Crowd*, pointed out as long ago as 1950 that in an "other-directed culture" the dominance of the family is supplanted by the peer group, and that its ethos, first operating on the child, persists into adulthood. What has this ethos to do with language in general and so with writing in particular? Lois DeBakey traces the connection.

The academic values adopted by peers usually affect school achievement. Adolescents generally rate the star athlete higher than the class "brain," and few schoolchildren emulate the scholar. The overachiever in school is, in fact, likely to have uncertain status among his peers. Children soon learn that being popular is more advantageous than being well-informed or literate. If "turning on" is "cool" and being a bookworm is "tacky," the choice is simple. When peer leadership derives from street wisdom, "hip" talk, arrogance, precocious pubescence, age, and size, an illiterate child may become an authority figure among his peers, and members of his group are not likely to strive for scholastic excellence. Antagonism to learning and animosity toward teachers are, indeed, sometimes requisites for peer approval. . . .

For generations, adolescents and young adults have used a private slang among peers, presumably to permit communication among themselves while excluding others. Teenage language today, however, is marked by an unusual amount of "hip" slang (What a ho-ho he is!) and ethnic slang (moxie, schlemiel, chutzpah, zilch; ciao; foxy lady, funky, jiving; macho, looking good!, que pasa?), as well as profanity and obscenity. Much teenage slang is also derived from the drug culture (dusted out, spaced out, bummer, blow your mind).[2]

So evanescent, so insubstantial is this slang that many of the words and phrases cited here are already outmoded or becoming so.

We make no plea for purism: slang and in-group lingo, however transient, however inexact, ugly, or opaque, is a normal, continuing human invention. The difficulty arises when high cultural value is assigned to the in-group vocabulary, a value that works against, indeed degrades, the value of Standard English. The difficulty is compounded when children, dominated by the authority of their friends, assume that the in-group's oral rhetoric may be freely used in formal writing and will remain intelligible, to themselves and others, five or ten years later.

The Media

In certain educational circles the utterance of the word television starts a quick flow of blood to the head. Whenever this occurs it is helpful to recall a famous passage from Plato's *Phaedrus*. Socrates tells Phaedrus about Theuth, a legendary god who discovered (among other arts) the use of letters. Theuth recommended to Thamus, King of Egypt, the adoption of the newfangled invention called writing. It would, he urged, make Egyptians both wiser and longer-memoried. To which King Thamus replied,

> this discovery of yours will create forgetfulness in the learners' souls, because they will not use their memories; they will trust to the external written characters and not remember of themselves. The specific which you have discovered is an aid not to memory, but to reminiscence, and you give your disciples not truth, but only the semblance of truth; they will be hearers of many things and will have learned nothing; they will appear to be omniscient and will generally know nothing; they will be tiresome company, having the show of wisdom without the reality.[3]

Thamus is the spokesman for the Platonic theory of ideas. This doctrine states that *all* representation, writing included, is no more than an imitation or faint reflection of the ideas, true and eternal, filed away somewhere in some heavenly cabinet. Unless we accept this odd but curiously persistent notion, Socrates' attack on writing loses its force. Still, it is salutary, when we are tempted to cry for the abolition of television, to remind ourselves that Socrates felt similarly about writing. He meant it too; like Jesus, he left us not a single word from his stylus. We owe our knowledge of him to his disobedient disciples, such scribblers as Plato and Xenophon.

Writing is probably here to stay. The question is, Who is to do it and how well? Television is also here to stay. With respect to it the questions are, What are the effects of television on writing? If bad, how can we mitigate these effects? If at all good, how can we profit from them?

The extreme case against the medium is expounded in *Four Arguments for the Elimination of Television*, by Jerry Mander.[4] His analysis is intricate and sophisticated; it dispenses with the familiar hand-wringing.

One can eliminate an institution, such as chattel slavery, when the social and economic structures underlying it change. But—as Jerry Mander must know—we probably cannot eliminate a universally accepted mode of communication, which is what television now is, no less than talking, writing, and gesturing.

Someone has said that, as with gas or electricity, the natural state of television is Off. We are now witnessing a transition into another state, which is beginning to seem equally natural: television as permanently On. The mere advocacy of its elimination (and by an ex-advertising man to boot) gives evidence of the tremendous actual and potential power of the medium. As we have seen, Socrates had the same premonition regarding the potentialities of the written word. His fears have proved gloriously unwarranted, and we may hope that Mr. Mander's fear will prove no less so. (The optimists among us may take comfort from the fact that in 1905 a Paris bookseller's quarterly announced that "the French no longer read—it is all the fault of the bicycle.")

At the moment, however, television's effect on oral and written language troubles all but a small group of electronic-age futurists and that much larger group for whom the effect is simply not a live issue. Our particular concern here is with the observable influence of television on literacy, and so on writing.

That influence has been intensively studied by Dr. DeBakey, whose conclusions are summarized in part below.[5]

Because television stresses immediacy and diversion, the child, making a natural transfer, expects education to be similarly immediate and diverting. Thus "by the time a child enters school, his attention span may be abbreviated to a few minutes or less." Writing, alas, makes infinitely greater demands on attention. Similarly, the high *visibility* of television conditions the child against the naked printed word, so that many children "have difficulty understanding a story that is not illustrated." The effect on learning to write is obvious. "Is it any wonder," asks DeBakey, "that children, after satisfying their physiologic and psychologic needs with instant information, instant pleasure, and instant food, balk at school assignments like writing," that require prolonged effort for mastery?

Along with this shortening of attention span goes a certain confusion as to what the attention is actually directed *to*. Seeing is believing, especially among the very young. Television entertainment, particularly when it turns on violence, may actually blur the difference between reality and artificially constructed images. "The person who cannot distinguish fake from fact may become indifferent to the value of truth, and an indifference to truth is inimical to accurate, objective exposition."

Dr. DeBakey also points out television's role as the provider of life models. Being worldly wise, like so many of television's child actors, "seems more appealing than being literate." The screen's misrepresentation of the classroom induces children to "consider it 'cool' to affect the contempt for books flaunted by [television's] fictitious class leaders." They will adopt *as standard usage* the street language spoken on a crime show or such a redundancy as in the commercial "Raid kills bugs dead."

Some newscasters are able to read quite clearly from reasonably well-written copy. But the majority of small stations employ men and women who cannot even pronounce the dreadful prose written for them. In 1978 the Unicorn Society of Lake Superior State College issued its Very Unique Redundancy Repetitive Award for the previous year. It cited such newscasters' favorites as "completely destroyed," "most unique," "more unique." It also cited, as part of its "dishonor list," such pronunciations (very common) as "nuk-u-lar" and such gobbledygook as "medication" for medicine, "the wet pavement situation" (it rained) and "the eating process." The problem is less that these particular phrases will be accepted by the student as imitable English as that they stand for a systematic and organized *style* of shoddy, dishonest expression. This style is being exploited day after day, 365 days a year. The composition class is at work only a couple of hours a week, if that.

What it comes down to is that English teachers are part of a market. They are competing with another language, one whose vulgarity, hollowness, impermanence, and low-grade capacity to communicate are equalled only by its immediate power to attract. They are not only teaching *toward* Standard English, they are teaching *against* another kind of English, one that—their environment being identical with that of their students—is also part of their own world of words and ideas.

The fact of this rivalry does not compel the conclusion that the English teacher alone is obliged to warn students against television's manipulation of their minds. That manipulation goes far beyond the merely linguistic; it is social, political, ethical, emotional, even religious. A delicate question arises: if, as may be the case, the *general*, though not exclusive, trend of television runs counter to the aims of education, should it not be the duty of teachers in *every* field (notably social studies) to warn the young television addict? We merely present the question for discussion.

Unless we agree with Jerry Mander's conclusion that television's effect on the body and mind are inseparable from the viewing experience, we should also admit that television at times supplies both perfectly good models of spoken English and information that students can absorb and later use in their thinking and writing. The trouble is that "bad" television is often so much more interesting than "good" television, so dominating, so omnipresent, that any possible benefit, from the teacher's viewpoint, is pretty well neutralized.

Turning now to the other media, we can safely say that radio is a less influential medium. Its effect on children's literacy and so on writing is perhaps subtler. Disc jockey jargon is quite defensible as a minor "in" language. But when the hearer confuses it with or prefers it to Standard English, trouble arises. To the young, radio is essentially a medium for music. No one demands that they change their tastes. But the relation of pop music and pop lyrics to language, though impalpable, is disturbing. The dominating sound, accompanied by the incoherent vocabulary of the purposely mumbled lyrics, tends to humiliate the mother tongue and reduce the prestige of Standard English. The relationship between the vivid world of radio noise and the quiet world of orderly written communication can be discerned only with difficulty.

Newspapers and magazines offer better models. Students can profit from exposure to such journalistic masters as Art Buchwald and Russell Baker and sports writers Red Smith and Jim Murray. But, as suggested earlier, the general quality of news-column English and magazine writing is declining. The cause of this decline is complex. In part it goes back to the employment of the half-educated, in part to a probably unconscious desire to compete with the "forcefulness" and stylishness of television.

The movies, despite many creditable achievements, suffer from the domination of television. They reflect a frantic desire to imitate television's modishness as well as an exaltation of street culture characters and the lingo proper to them. One interesting consequence of the demand for action is that the sound track is often incomprehensible, as in the popular *Star Wars*. Speech itself (which may be quite effective, clear English) is degraded, placed in an inferior position. We are not reverting to silent movies, but rather passing into an era of movies accompanied by baffling noise presented as though it were real talk. The effect on the student's own feeling for language cannot be good. It is to their visual nature that films owe their power to attract. This fact has not been overlooked by certain educators, whose thinking reflects the current ascendancy of the visual image over the written word. In 1975 the editor of *English Today* suggested that courses be given in "Creative Writing without Words" and "A Visual Approach to Writing." Egyptian hieroglyphic notation was once thought a primitive form of communication. We are now urged to return to it.

It is hard to estimate the effect of (noncurricular) book reading on the literacy of young people. Children's literature is livelier and more varied than it has ever been and probably contains no more trash than in past periods. The new naturalistic school of children's book writers, however, exploits street language and vogue lingo on the grounds that these forms reflect the way children talk. To some extent this assumption is true. It is also true that the net effect is the reinforcement of questionable linguistic habits. Older children, reading such moderns as Kurt Vonnegut, are apt to imitate in their own writing the eccentricities and inelegancies that the author has for stylistic reasons purposely exploited, but which the unsophisticated reader may swallow—hook, line, and sinker—as models for general imitation. In general, however, it is better for the student to read books of almost *any* quality than to read none at all. One's taste can always be improved, but it must start from *something*.

Adult Models

Any list of environmental pressures that act on the student's desire and ability to write must include adult models. At age eight the writer of these lines idolized prize fighters. He would much rather have been Johnny Kilbane than Woodrow Wilson. Had this idolatry endured, he might now be passing out towels in a run-down training gym. His interests shifted to books and writers, and so he became a word-handler. The reader will have to judge whether this outcome has been of any benefit to society. The point is that in 1912 the social environment favored such a shift in interest. A prize fighter, though enjoying a certain limited, well-deserved prestige, was not generally hailed as a culture hero, but the traditional respect accorded in the classroom to "authors" was as yet unchallenged. The point is that a child's willingness to learn writing, and thus his eventual ability to write, is in great part a function of those attitudes toward writing he sees evinced by society.

We know that the language of professionals in general has a way of filtering down and reappearing in the teenager's written prose. A college-bound student, shopping in the supermarket of college catalogues, may come across this description of a writing course (the example is drawn from Dr. DeBakey's inexhaustible treasury of horrors):

> This course will examine both oral and written communication and various other interactions between members of the health team and their clients in respect to various therapeutic and operational conditions. The technique of writing clear,

concise, and pertinent instructions, reports and documents, in order to optimize the clients [sic] therapeutic experience will be examined and developed in detail. It is anticipated that material covered in this course will not be limited to intrahospital dialogues but will be extended to interactions with the clients [sic] families, and various other community agencies and institutions.[6]

The student reading such prose will normally assume that it represents the way to write—after all, it describes a course in writing.

Bureaucrats and politicians have not, since Richard Nixon's high drama, been held in high esteem by our youth. You might find a boy or girl who would like to be president, but for the most part our young people look elsewhere for their gods. Still, the bureaucrats and politicians speak and write accepted, respected, but obscure lingos that pervade the media and thereby become a noxious gas inevitably inhaled by young people. Thus it is, according to Dr. DeBakey, that many a student composition reflects an uneasy marriage between such trendy phrases as "I'm really *into* stuffed cabbage" and the pathetic lexicon of officialdom: *viable, dialogue, relevant, dichotomy, credibility gap, prioritize. . . .*

But if youth's real heroes are not politicians or educators, who are they? They are sports and entertainment figures. The two groups are now merged in show business, thanks to the media, which inexorably make sports a fiefdom of commercial entertainment.

The August 1976 issue of the *Ladies Home Journal* published the results of a poll of several hundred students in grades 5–12:

Girls' Top Ten Heroes and Heroines

1. O. J. Simpson
2. Neil Armstrong
3. Robert Redford
4. Elton John
5. Billie Jean King
6. Mary Tyler Moore
7. John Wayne
8. Chris Evert
9. Katharine Hepburn
10. Henry Kissinger

Boys' Top Ten Heroes and Heroines

1. O. J. Simpson
2. Elton John
3. John Wayne
4. Chris Evert
5. Neil Armstrong

6. Joe Namath
7. Henry Kissinger
8. Robert Redford
9. Gerald Ford
10. Mary Tyler Moore

Of those listed only Kissinger, Ford, and Armstrong do not belong to the world of sports and entertainment—and Armstrong and Kissinger were, of course, both promoted in orthodox show-biz fashion. Now no one would expect an eighteen-year-old to choose the playwright Samuel Beckett for his or her hero. The issue is subtler. It turns on the fact that the whole world of feeling (and therefore of expression) represented by sports and entertainment is accepted by many young people as the sole or main one worthy of emulation. That world, quite properly, has little to do with literacy. The Drs. DeBakey, keeping in mind the difficulties created for the English teacher by these idols of the tribe, put the case this way:

> . . . a prize fighter who flaunts his disregard for standard English by spewing ungrammatical boasts and nonsensical doggerel earned $15 million in a single year; he has been honored at the White House, lionized the world over, and awarded honorary degrees. . . . An unschooled female country singer with a succession of gold records has par-layed her ungrammatical speech into a fortune, enhanced by royalties from a best-selling "autobiography" written in her rural vernacular.[7]

In a recent cartoon in *The Wall Street Journal* (September 7, 1977) a father's exhortation to his son mocks the modern route to "success": "Instead of a college education, I've bought you a guitar. Get out there and make a million bucks."[8]

We are told that, for children to talk and write competently, they should be immersed in, surrounded by, language. Well and good. But if a fair part of what they are immersed in is the animal whine, the gutter gutturals of the rock star, what then? And if this rock star, as is reported of Peter Frampton, made $50 million in one year and is, naturally enough, accorded semidivine status by his young hearers, what then? Over the centuries our language has submitted to all kinds of authority, a circumstance that displeases language libertarians. But was yesterday's Elvis Presley a happier influence on English than yesteryear's much derided schoolmarm?

In the final analysis, the powerful authority emanating from the sacred Olympus of sports and entertainment induces many a student to substitute diversion for education. How are educators to combat this situation? In a despairing letter to the *Los Angeles Times* a North Dakota teacher writes, "Try as I might, I cannot make correct spelling into a comedy routine."

The idolization of the superbowl and the superstar tends to modify the curriculum itself. A high school music course is often no more than the meeting of the school band, basically a servant of school sports. Some schools give credit for cheerleading, and one wonders how many thousands of compositions annually bear the title "My Favorite Movie Star." As modern entertainment in its wide range makes little or no demands on literacy (indeed can make profits by demeaning it), a school environment that imitates the "culture" of entertainment will tend to make fewer and fewer demands on what was once thought to be the distinguishing feature of mankind—articulate speech.

The Culture in General

Gutenberg began to develop his printing technique in 1438. It was thirty-five years before Caxton (in 1474) set up his press and revolutionized writing and reading in England.Today our communications technology transmits information almost instantaneously. In consequence, the impact on our behavior of all large, deep culture shifts is felt almost immediately. Writing is part of such behavior.

The culture shifts that involve writing are complex, and one must show caution in tying them to our present concern. But we may cite a few such shifts that teachers themselves tell us do actually show up in classroom work.

The forces at work are not separate or distinct, but mingled parts of a whole climate of thought and feeling. We put down on paper such catchwords and phrases as permissivism, antiintellectualism, cynical materialism, the emergence of an oral culture, and the dominance of the machine. But simultaneously we sense that all these elements are somehow one and the same, threads in a single web from which the fly of literacy struggles to free itself.

Writing is not a game. Nor is it a pleasure, though pleasure may follow the completion of a satisfactory sentence or paragraph. Writers do not "enjoy" writing; it is simply something their natures and talents require them to do. A "me generation"—obsessed with self—cannot conceive of writing except perhaps as a form of liberation. One student says, "I write so I can get my frustrations, or in some cases, happiness down on paper before I forget them." In itself this is not a bad sentence, and the feeling behind it is not unnatural or unworthy, but it is a feeling that does not reinforce the urge to learn. There is a great difference between students who write to *express* themselves and those who write to express their *selves.*

Similarly, an overindulgent or undisciplined society that devalues intellectual effort will also devalue approved language norms. When, on May 1, 1970, Abbie Hoffman announced to a crowd of students in a television broadcast, "We gotta redefine the fuckin' language," he was striking at the heart of the matter. If you can get people to use nonmental or antimental language, you have gone a long way toward anarchy. A. Bartlett Giamatti had that idea in mind when he stated that today's college students are the products of the "antistructures" of the late sixties and early seventies.[9] In consequence, for the first time in our national history, an education is no longer, for many students, a high priority.

In the sense that written words are structures, loose and vapid talk is an antistructure. Ours is a time that trusts talk; the "talk show" is a symbol of that trust. Now, a culture stressing "oracy," as against literacy, is not in itself dangerous. Risk ensues when oracy gains so much authority that a television interviewer whose mental powers are obviously not limitless can earn, or receive, $1 million a year. Risk also ensues when in a modern society an oral culture is not checked or balanced by a culture of the responsible written word.

In the foregoing sections we dwelt, with admitted superficiality, on some of the aspects of our culture that make the composition teacher's job harder. Our purpose has not been to indict society. It has been simply to suggest that though the road to literacy—or back to it—must and should start with institutional changes in the educational system, it must also take into account underlying social forces that move us all, including the teacher, the parent, and the writer of these lines.

Chapter 3

Why Write?

Why write? The question is not as absurd as it might seem. Today all is questioned: marriage, sex, religion, patriotism, the state, the need to work. Therefore it is no surprise to find education under attack, and with it literacy and that fixative of literacy called writing.

If the issue of writing interested only think-tank philosophers and cocktail-party conversationalists, there would be no need to write this chapter. But the issue has trickled down into the classroom. Teachers of writing who brood over unmotivated students are often up against something queerer than stupidity, hostility, or "lack of interest." They may be facing a more deeply rooted obstacle, the student's vague feeling that our time calls for writing no more than for Sanskrit. Because this negative attitude poses a problem in day-to-day teaching, we must consider the case against writing. Following that, we will turn to the case for it.

The Case against Learning to Write

The antis may be thought of under four main heads. Writing (meaning more than the ability to write one's name and fill out simple forms) is discredited on these grounds: it is of scant practical utility; it is being outmoded by cultural changes; requiring it as a skill denies personal freedom; and, except to superior students, it is, under present educational conditions, unteachable. Let's take these points in order.

Utility

In another era a practical pastime was any activity that helped you become a better developed and more interesting human being. Thus, the ability to sing, play bridge, or ride a horse was of practical utility, even though you had no hopes of becoming a professional singer, card player, or equestrian. Today, with the narrowing of our sense of life's possibilities, the meaning of the term practical has narrowed also; now it refers only to bread-winning.

The argument from utility is simple enough. It is that one can become enormously successful (rock stars, film stars, film magnates, Mafia millionaires) without being able to write competently. This statement is true, as it is no less true that such successful and honored citizens can always hire others to do their writing for them. (These others, of course, must somehow, somewhere have learned to write—but no matter.) Now look at the other end of the scale, where live the conspicuously *unsuccessful*. The vice president of the Sloan Foundation, Stephen White, tells us, "I doubt that a coal miner has any real need for writing skills, nor will his life be changed very much one way or another if he lacks them."[1]

Most of us, economically speaking, are to be found between the rock star and the coal miner. Even for this majority, runs the argument, the practical need to write diminishes proportionately with the growth of communications technology. Instructors at the University of California, Berkeley, wonder whether in an age of television and telephones it is still necessary to be able to write an essay. At a high-level conference held about a decade ago one perfectly intelligent educator, Miriam Wilt, argued, "Of those sixty out of a hundred young people who finally show up in Freshman Composition class, how many will ever need or wish to write again except for those interminable term papers? . . . Why spend all of this precious school time perfecting a skill that will seldom or never be used?" Even though the same question might be raised with respect to the teaching of mathematics, the sciences, history, and most other basic subjects, the generality of the question doesn't cancel out the need to answer it. But the argument from utility makes still another point: while the connection between the better-paying job and higher social status remains firm, social status itself is no longer enhanced by the ability to write. Writing has lost its prestige.

The Sound-and-Picture Culture

The argument from utility is based in part on the more general contention that technology is outmoding our traditional ways of communication. The culture as a whole is seen as turning away from the written and printed word and toward a new culture of signals emitted by the electronic media, film, computer, pocket calculator, and a host of devices still to come. Thus, we need only attain the minimum ability to read and write required by the new devices. In theory this ability might eventually disappear altogether, just as the art of illuminating manuscripts disappeared with the advent of movable type.

Basically, this belief in an evolving sound-and-picture culture is the essence of Marshall McLuhan's prophecy, which burst into prominence in the late sixties in *The Medium Is the Massage.* Many respectable educators echo this argument, or rather reflect its influence, though they would doubtless stop short of swallowing McLuhan whole. In NAEP's 1975 report the commentators note, for example, "a movement away from established conventions [we assume this means Standard English] toward those of spoken discourse." They point to "a growing . . . preference for visual communication," so that "routine writing may move toward simpler forms."

Tentatively, the commentators ask some interesting questions. They wonder about the actual meaning of the test results: "Scorers may prefer standards of written expression that are becoming outmoded. New standards are certainly different, but they may not be worse in any defensible sense." And they suggest a change in attitude that goes to the heart of the issue: a general call for a change in the assumptions held by educators and parents about the importance of writing skills in our culture.[2]

Those who accept the idea that a fundamental shift in modes of communication is taking place consider oracy at least a partial replacement of literacy. It can well be argued that Shakespeare "wrote for audiences, not for readers." In the May 1970 *Harvard Educational Review*, Neil Postman, a professor of English education at New York University, advocated the discontinuance of reading (and, logically, writing) in favor of "media literacy."

The emphasis on oracy is perhaps influenced by McLuhan's idea of the transformation of the world by technology into a "global village." In a village, formal written communication is not as appropriate as talk, the exchange of gossip. The crystallization of ideas and feelings we call writing seems somehow associated with the city rather than the hamlet. In any event, this second argument against writing stems from the perception of an emergent sound-and-picture culture and the judgment (or the fear) that it will prescribe the kinds of signals we send each other.

Personal Freedom

The contention of the third argument is quite simple: children should not be forced to learn against their will. With respect to literacy the contention is put positively: children have the right to their own language. If these two propositions are accepted, it follows that writing should be taught only to those who enjoy learning it and who also accept without qualification the primacy of Standard English. In that case many difficulties the English teacher now faces would evaporate. For one thing, classes would be much smaller. For another, the discipline problem would vanish, along with the students. Indeed, the principle of personal freedom, if implemented, would rid us of so many of our troubles that the temptation to embrace it should be strong. One is surprised that at the moment it is making so little headway.

The dogma of child freedom has a mixed origin. Partly it is the residue of an early twentieth-century misunderstanding or distortion of John Dewey's theories of progressive education. George Weber puts it this way:

> Another idea, growing out of progressive education, was that it was authoritarian (and hence undemocratic) for the school and the teacher to exercise authority over the child. The *child* should decide what he wanted to study and the school should serve his "felt needs." The teacher should become a passive advisor, a resource person. This notion was physically expressed in getting the teacher away from the front of the classroom.[3]

But the argument from the idea of personal freedom was more decisively shaped by a major tenet of the youth movement of the 1960s: do your own thing. It was given even firmer footing by the weakening of home discipline, reflected, naturally enough, in the child's rebellious attitude in the classroom. Finally, it rooted itself in a general uneasy feeling that, as a world of lunatic violence, killing, and pollution seemed to offer no particularly bright future to our children, they might at least have the pleasure of doing what they wanted. Such desperate hedonism might lead to an actual refusal to be educated. Today indignant generals and government leaders cannot understand the memoranda produced by their underlings. Would they not be astonished if told that the trouble may have some connection with My Lai, Hiroshima, and the napalming of children in Indochina? A passion for destruction, history shows us, rarely goes along with a passion for learning.

Defeatism

The final argument against writing results from the conviction, held by many teachers and educational experts, that our era's violent changes—demographic, ethnic, and socioeconomic— have uncovered or created a large number of unteachables. It is best, they say, to admit this fact and encourage the school to develop its merely custodial function. Writing is for a superior, mandarin group. As some queen of Spain is reputed to have remarked in connection with an even more widespread practice, it is too good for the common people.

This view may be rooted in an unconscious fear and hatred of "the rabble"—a fear and hatred probably alive in all of us, including the rabble. It has been voiced a thousand times, and in our century, for example, by the idolized novelist D. H. Lawrence: "The great mass of the population should never be taught to read and write. Never." (One of the most remarkable statements ever made by a man who lived largely on his royalties.) Since those who hold an elitist attitude are by necessity members of the majority ethnic group, it is safe to assume that a certain amount of unconscious racism probably informs the defeatist attitude—the notion that Blacks, Chicanos, Italians, Poles are by nature incapable of learning how to read or write properly. Jacques Barzun puts the point in perspective:

> Still more unjust to youth is the assumption that "background" permits or prevents the learning of such rudiments as reading and writing—as if this country had not been peopled and developed by millions whose ancestors did *not* read and write. The fact is, reading and writing themselves

were *invented by illiterates*—and since that time every person of normal mind can be brought to share that heritage.[4]

It is fair to say, however, that most of those who throw up their hands are not racists or elitists or rabble-haters. They are simply of the opinion that our present social chaos, the sudden increase in the school population, and the apparent decrease in teaching competence all combine to make universal literacy impossible. Some really believe that many young Americans, regardless of class or color, are unteachable, while others merely feel that, given the obstacles the teacher faces, it is not feasible to try to teach all of them how to write.

So much for the four arguments against writing. The child, who has a right to his own language, would put the question more succinctly: *Wotsinit f'me? Writin' is nuts. Ida wanna. I can't.*

We turn now to a point-by-point rebuttal of the arguments presented here. In doing so we mean to build the opposite case, thereby convincing our readers of the value of writing and of our great need as a civilization for maintaining it as a skill accessible to everyone.

The Case for Writing

Utility

We might start our rebuttal with Stephen White's coal miner. First, he wasn't a coal miner when at age six he learned to write. True, his later life gave him little chance to use that skill. Indeed, being "overqualified" may have handicapped him in getting a job in his chosen line. But the school, despite all the responsibilities it is asked to assume, it not as yet required to be a crystal-gazer. It is still charged with the democratic duty of educating *all* citizens so as to give them some chance to find a job in accordance with their interests and capacities. We are not in truth a classless society, but at least the classifying should not start in the classroom.

Furthermore, can one seriously argue that, because an illiterate coal miner may be able to survive, writing must vanish from the curriculum? Americans are disinclined to settle for mere physical survival. And, beyond that, the word *survival* itself, in a complex culture such as ours, has a different meaning than it would in a community of savages.

The fact is, the only acceptable sense of *survival* includes the concept of leading a moderately decent life, and today this stipulation involves *more* writing than in past periods. Ours is not a fixed society, like that of the feudal period, with few needs and sparse intercourse. Ours is a vibrating, constantly changing world that entails mutual dependence, shifts of status and dwelling, and increasing communication with government on all levels. Charles Scribner puts it this way:

> In spite of the increased use of the spoken word, there must always be a need for the written word—a word that must also be read: instructions and messages that must be given and understood accurately in the home, in stores, at work, and on the highway. It is most unlikely that recorded announcements however ubiquitous, or pictorial signs however ingenious, will make it any less necessary to learn reading and writing than cars make it unnecessary to learn how to walk. For most purposes the written word retains unique advantages: it is cheap, convenient, effective, and (when need be) intensely personal and private.
>
> There are innumerable occasions when writing is inescapable: job applications, insurance claims, consumer inquiries, approaches to strangers, letters of condolence, recommendation, technical advice—and love. Young men and women owe it to themselves—to say nothing of their families—to be able to fulfill these requirements and obtain these adjuncts of self-development. The fact that illiterate persons can "survive" is a poor argument in a society concerned with the quality of life.[5]

Without cease, then, we signal to each other. What is the consequence? "What we are noticing," comments Aidan Chambers, "is that people—just to live their normal lives—now need greater skills as speakers, readers, and writers than they have ever needed before."[6]

Looking further, past survival, we see that writing competence is in most cases essential for practical achievement and in many situations a decisive advantage. In which fields of activity will current students find their livelihood? Less than 5 percent of our population produces food and fiber; less than 25 percent is engaged in manufacturing. The growing area appears to be mutual service, that enormous web of activities making possible the distribution of goods, both material and impalpable. This web is held together by words, some spoken, many written. If this were not so, the service industries would not be making so many complaints about inadequate writing. The media, especially film and television, will continue to grow, with a consequent demand for those who can handle words efficiently and clearly.

The argument for the practical utility of writing is buttressed by the whole drift of our economy. Whether that drift is in a good direction is beside the point. We're in it—and the improvement of society will itself depend partly on writing.

The Sound-and-Picture Culture

No one denies either the power or the popularity of the audiovisual environment. No one denies—or for that matter, decries—whatever enrichment our written language may derive from that environment, as long as it *is* enrichment and not impoverishment. No sensible teacher of writing holds up for rigid emulation any model of the classical tradition's formal style. Ours is not an Addisonian age, and it is absurd to pretend that it is.

Accordingly, we take the common-sense view that peaceful coexistence not only may, but inevitably will, obtain between a sound-and-picture culture, however aggressive, and a written-word culture, however threatened. The advent of the printed book, whose impact in a smaller world was quite comparable to television's in our larger one, did not destroy the art of formal, persuasive speech, though it did make some inroads on that of simple conversation.

The developing countries that most eagerly adopt the new media are also the ones careful to send their best young people to Western universities, where they eagerly absorb the tradition of literacy. Third-world countries understand perhaps better than we do that the technoculture has increased the output of written signals. The so-called communications and knowledge explosion is simply the continuing proliferation of signals of *all* kinds. The expansion of knowledge cannot be handled only by electronic data banks. At the beginning of the process stands—first in thought, then on the page—the Word. Whatever influence Marshall McLuhan at one time exerted flowed not from any oral arguments but from those in his books, written in conventional English prose. Anyone eager to hear about the death of the book had to read one.

What the philosophers say, however, means less than what big business does in this regard. The last decade or so has seen the takeover, by the airlords and such vast companies as Xerox, of trade publishing houses, textbook firms, and magazines. If the written word were dying, would these shrewd judges of profit potential so joyfully invest their capital in it? Our present production of thirty-six thousand books a year hardly suggests the deathbed.

If we restrict our gaze to what is happening in the schools (remembering, however, that we are a bandwagon people) we note an increasing disillusionment with sound-and-picture pedagogy, play-party "happenings," and "activity learning," and a return to paper, pencil, book, and that oddly persistent human habit, the operation known as *thinking*.

Personal Freedom

In answer to the argument for personal freedom we merely note, without making too much of it, the obvious fact that the exaltation of the self, so popular in the sixties, has spent its force or transformed itself into social movements (such as women's liberation) that are based on reasonable grounds. Not that anyone demands a return to the classroom discipline of fifty years ago, for we have learned how unnatural that was. What parents and increasingly the students themselves are now requesting is simply an atmosphere in which essential studies can be pursued efficiently and not unpleasantly. They seem to be proceeding on the notion that the freedom *to* choose from a full range of possibilities, as well as the freedom *from* ignorance and illiteracy, both depend on a knowledge of reading and writing. As the whole purpose of this book is to demonstrate that writing belongs among these few essential studies, we for the moment let the issue of personal freedom rest.

Defeatism

With respect to the defeatism argument—that certain people are simply unteachable—both faith and works are involved.

To throw up one's hands in despair is to express a faith—the faith of antifaith. True unbelievers feel that, for whatever reasons, many children are *intrinsically* unable to learn to write in more than a primitive sense. To this antifaith we oppose the equally dogmatic faith expressed in the introduction to this book: *We believe that every normal Jane and Johnny can, if properly taught, learn how to write clearly and correctly.*

"If properly taught" is the escape clause leading from faith to works. "They cannot be taught" is not the same as "we don't know how to teach them." Writing is not, like higher mathematics, a discipline only the favored mind can master. Though it differs significantly from speech, writing is an accessible variant of an operation, using easily learned symbols, that is built into our biological structure. It may be that great or "natural" writers are born rather than taught. But competent writers, building upon the language sense that appears to distinguish us as a species from other animals, can be trained by instruction and practice.

As our whole discussion should make clear, the impediments to this learning process are many, but none is in theory unremovable. Institutional changes can be made if we really want to make them—and we may find that such changes will decrease rather than increase our tax bill, especially if we resolve to rid our schools of time-wasting electives. The social pressures outlined in Chapter 2 are not irreversible; they can be combated. And in the struggle we may find, as time goes on, both parents and children moving to our side of the fence. But the defeatist attitude will evaporate, after all, only if we teach well and the results become apparent. Chapters 5 and 6 deal, we hope helpfully, with the learning and teaching of writing.

In fact, present controversy over methods may be a good thing. It may be that we shall have to start from scratch, as the pioneers did when they settled beyond the Alleghenies. There is something wholesome and bracing, rather than doleful, in this quiet statement by W. Dean Memering: "Inevitably we are forced to admit that no one really knows how composition should be taught. There are nine and seventy ways, and all of them are wrong—or right if you prefer."[7] Memering does not say that writing can't be taught—indeed he is full of suggestions that assume it can—but simply that we should learn how to teach it. The present atmosphere of serious research, the return to methods of instruction so old that they seem new, some of the teacher-training projects mentioned in Chapter 7—all point to a growing willingness on the part of teachers to find out how to teach better. If this trend can be matched by increased willingness of students to learn, we will still be far from a utopia of literacy, but we will at least have discomfited the defeatists.

The Defense on Political Grounds

Two more points concern us, and to them the antiwriting contingent have no matching arguments.

Let us examine two quotations in the light of each other:

The tendency of democracies is, in all things, to mediocrity.[8]

We must recognize the importance of critical thought in any discipline and the special role it plays in developing a society's communication skills; and we must acknowledge the intimate tie between true critical thought and democracy: The absence of one always signals the demise of the other, and all too often we appreciate neither until both disappear.[9]

These two statements of belief (not of demonstrable fact) by James Fenimore Cooper and Daniel Shanahan flatly contradict each other. The defense of literacy in general and writing in particular stands or falls as you adhere to one or the other. If we are *fated* to mediocrity, the efficient thing is to settle for minimum universal literacy, or perhaps even literacy for an elite minority. But if Shanahan is right, the kind of government most of us believe in depends in some measure on the clear use of words, for without such use, "true critical thought" is impossible. Mr. Shanahan, as he well knows, is not saying anything new. He is repeating what the inventors of democracy, the ancient Greeks (though, as slaveholders and male chauvinists, they had a restricted idea of it), knew twenty-five hundred years ago. Charles Scribner puts the case clearly:

> It is not farfetched to attribute the peculiar vigor of Greek intellectual life to the influence and stimulus of their written traditions. It is as though the practice of writing increased their love of the language, their awareness of the power of words, and their passion for rational thought.

One of the tentative conclusions reached by commentators on the NAEP report is that there seems to be on all age levels (though less so among thirteen-year-olds) a polarization of good and bad writers. Such a polarization has to some extent always existed, presumably it always will, but of recent years, despite the current reaction in favor of writing, the polarization appears to be intensifying. Such a shift entails a political danger—the possibility that two classes of writers, barbarians and mandarins, will emerge. Such class petrifaction is in direct contradiction to our democratic notions.

It is too easy to say that writing is thinking. But it is fair to say that because writing is a more difficult activity than casual talking, writing exacts more thought, just as working with a brush, pencil, or crayon exacts more effort than fingerpainting or hurling pigments upon canvas.

The thread that binds "true critical thought" and the operation of writing has been well studied by Ronald Berman, formerly head of the National Endowment for the Humanities. He writes that

> writing . . . is the fundamental mode of learning. . . . Writing is a series of conceptual decisions. Even within fiction it must describe, include, select, compare, define and ascribe, among many other logical responsibilities. It moves from evidence, through reasoning, to conclusion. It can do these things in a thousand different ways, indirect as poetry, heavy as the law. But it does after all have to translate feeling and intuition into statement and that procedure underlies everything in the life of the mind.

There is, of course, a second, and less methodological reason for writing: One never knows what he knows until it is written. That is to say, until the individual engages himself, fights the most primary of intellectual battles, until he argues with his creativity he cannot formulate that creativity. Far from "expressing" the self, what writing does is allow judgment of the self. That is why it is a *critical* procedure, and why it is so important as a form of free play to say nothing of imposed educational work.[10]

The National Assessment of Education Progress recently reported the results of some tests taken by teenagers. Among seventeen-year-olds one out of four could not explain the basic concept of democracy—that we elect our leaders. Fifty-eight percent of thirteen-year-olds failed the question. Fewer than half the teenagers could name even one of their senators or representatives in Congress. The NAEP report attributed this lack of information to the growing unpopularity of civics courses and the burgeoning of electives. The whole explanation is probably more wide-ranging. Still, many electives do *not* require writing, whereas courses in government or history do—or should. The connection between writing and the polling booth may not seem direct, but it is real. From the inception of the republic, the idea that education and democracy are linked has been part of our tradition. Education without literacy is meaningless. The capacity to read without the capacity to write is almost equally so. In fact, a fair goal might be to reach a national level of literacy at which all citizens are able to write letters to their representatives in Congress. The case for writing, therefore, rests in part on political grounds, on the sense of duty and gratitude we feel as citizens of a free country. It is put concisely by the motto of a recent one-cent stamp: The Ability to Write· A Root of Democracy.

The Growth of the Individual

The final defense of writing, as of reading, depends on our conception of a developed human being. That in turn depends on the kind of culture we are talking about. A preliterate or nonliterate culture can produce superior human beings—superior, that is, in terms of the ideals of that culture. Ulysses, for example, was undeniably superior. But with us the die is cast. Our civilization not only requires literacy but uses it as a tool for its own advancement. Stored memory is our number one tool; we are helpless without it. Words and the ideas they express are essential to the energetic mental life on which are based the performance and progress of our particular society. This mental life cannot be entirely passive; all of us, as writers, readers, thinkers, must within the limits of our capacity engage actively in it. "Language is learned," says one educator, "not because we want to talk or read or write about language, but because we want to talk and read and write about the world."[11]

Thus, the final argument for writing has to do with the impoverishment or the enrichment of the human spirit. We do not plead primarily for the creation of Ernest Hemingways or Rebecca Wests. We plead only for "decent writing" (Jacques Barzun's phrase) because it is one method (among others) of establishing a clearer understanding of the relation between the individual and the world. It is a mode of self-judgment and a mode of understanding the not-self. It is thus, in the finer sense of the word, practical.

Mr. Barzun states,

What is the universal necessity for decent writing?

First, *to increase accuracy.* Misunderstanding is easy and natural; carrying the right idea out of one skull into another is hard and unnatural.

Second, *to economize attention.* All of us suffer from the bombardment of stimuli and the shortness of time. The Chief Justice said that if every night the bench must read a brief of 216 pages, the work of the Court would so pile up as to defeat justice altogether.

Third, *to clarify individual opinion.* Anyone who writes even passably well knows what he thinks far better than one who does not write or writes badly. The act of writing is a task of *sorting out,* which helps to eliminate foolishness, prejudice, inconsistency, and dull clichés.

Fourth, *to speed up action.* This hardly needs comment after what officials tell us about their own rules and what citizens endure as a result. All of us are perpetually filling out forms or trying to follow written directions. Each operation takes twice or three times as long as it should on account of bad writing.

Fifth, *to see through fraud, deceit, propaganda.* Whoever writes well has learned to scan words for meanings hidden and overt and will automatically detect the rhetorical tricks by which irrelevancies and gaps in logic are concealed or made plausible.

Sixth, *to extend and make more subtle the enjoyment from human communication.* There is no need to argue for what is as great a pleasure as music or painting. But why do I list it under necessity? Simply because without more pleasure of the sort that words afford we stand a good chance, not of building Babel, but much sooner of going down a steep place like the Gadarene swine.[12]

Chapter 4

What Is Writing?

The connection between spoken and written communication is not only basic but mutually nourishing. The good teacher of written composition should also be an adequate model of oral English and should ask of the students clear, economical speech. But speaking and writing are far from interchangeable. In part because the electronic media confer such high status on talk, some teachers tend to encourage the student to "write naturally—just the way you'd say it." One can sympathize with this counsel. Were students to follow it, the effect would be to lighten the teachers' workload. The result, however, would not be competent writing.

Oral and written language differ in one crucial respect, as important as it is obvious. When we talk, we are part of a living situation involving others actually present. The effect of what we say is achieved not only by the meaning and arrangement of the uttered words but also by the expectations of the audience, whether a group or an individual. We also convey our meaning and make an effect through gesture and facial expression, especially that of the eye; through variations of volume, tone, pitch, and stress; through silences; and even through errors, sloppy usages, and diction not suited to the written page. Conversation is thick with clues and signals that reinforce the content of the words, often supplying meaning when the words themselves are lacking, poorly chosen, or clumsily arranged. What little we were permitted to hear of the Nixon tapes taught the whole nation this lesson.

Writing, on the other hand, is a kind of premeditated speech. Even in its simplest form, it involves acute self-consciousness. Furthermore, it depends only upon itself. It does not take place in a person-to-person context. It must convey its message clearly and completely to one or more persons. Once edited, written material is inflexible. As we talk we are continually shading, correcting, expanding, bettering (or, it may be, worsening) our fluid statements. But written communication cannot rely on such assistance. To achieve its end, therefore, it uses a different set of tools: the disciplines of composition and the rules of syntax, grammar, spelling, punctuation, and paragraphing.

We are not here arguing for a specialized vocabulary, dressed-up language, or a self-conscious style. Indeed, some of the ease, flow, and spontaneity of conversation reappears in certain kinds of writing. A Mark Twain, an Ernest Hemingway admirably exploits the rhythms and idioms of the spoken tongue. But such cunning artists know just how far to go and how to make these rhythms and idioms meet the requirements of a reader, not a listener. The impression, as of a unique voice overheard, that we receive from some of the poems of Robert Frost or the essays of Charles Lamb is carefully contrived. Such writing is not simply a transcription of real talk. It is to the ear what *trompe l'oeil* painting is to the eye. Written records transcribed from audio tapes of spontaneous remarks or the minutes of a business conference usually make painful reading. The tape recorder is an ethical as well as a technical device. It is a master teacher of humility.

In other words, even at its most informal, writing, as contrasted with talking, is bound by certain conventions. These conventions help us to communicate clearly when gestures, facial expression, and so forth are not available to help us. In *The Philosophy of Composition*, E. D. Hirsch gives an example when he discusses "the convention in writing that sentences shall normally be grammatically complete, with both an explicit subject and an explicit predicate." This convention may be, and often quite properly is, ignored in conversation. That is why, as Hirsch states, "for native speakers the chief difficulty in learning to write well is in learning how to use language in an unaccustomed way. The functional peculiarity of writing is its need to furnish its own context."[1]

Precisely because it uses language "in an unaccustomed way," writing is best learned in a more formal environment than that in which by some happy miracle of nature we all learn to talk. To equate the two forms of expression is, however tempting, to shortchange the student.

But if writing is not talk on paper, what is it? Filling in a multiple-choice test involves a kind of writing. So does the creation of *Hamlet*. Among other features distinguishing these two kinds of writings, one is pertinent to our discussion: the first kind can be taught and learned; the second cannot be. In a sense the first is not writing at all, but *marking*. The second is of so special a kind as to be beyond the concerns of the composition (though not the literature) class. At some point between these two extremes lies the writing that interests us. If for the moment we think only in terms of quality, we can very roughly identify three varieties: survival writing, competent writing, and superior writing.

Survival Writing

Using a cliché that reflects certain failures in our whole society, we call the first kind of writing on our list survival writing.* Survival writing goes beyond multiple-choice marking. It includes, we may suppose, the ability to put down legibly at least the following: one's name, address, sex, hair and eye color, weight, height, religious affiliation if any, phone number, Social Security number, names of parents or next of kin, bank or other reference, the digits in various combinations, the date, the days of the week, the months of the year, and so forth. Survival writing probably includes the ability to commit to paper, with excusable misspellings, a few thousand of the commonest English words, including a few proper names and geographical nouns, together with a minimum capacity to manipulate this vocabulary in short, understandable sentences. Survival writers should be able to record a telephone message and fill out common forms—assuming that they can understand them, which is not apt to be the case with insurance policies or income-tax forms. Survival writers also should be able to write a brief job-application letter, free of errors. This talent may be superfluous, however, since the very idea of a survival society assumes the acceptance of permanent and increasing unemployment.

---

*A term proposed by George Weber is *survival education*, which he defines as "a kind of competence-based education designed to give students the minimum practical skills and knowledge necessary for 'survival' in contemporary society. Tends to emphasize specific applied skills such as keeping a checkbook, filling out common forms, finding names in a telephone directory, making change, personal hygiene, and swimming." From George Weber, *Back to Basics in the Schools* (unpublished manuscript), p. 200.

Survival writers should be able to make legible lists of the goods they normally consume. Their vocabulary should be sufficient to enable them to write brief but comprehensible letters required at certain important moments in life: for example, advising distant relatives of a death in the family, requesting a job reference, requesting a transcript of school grades, and so forth.

Perhaps it will be admitted that this much, even in our present condition of educational disarray, can be taught to all normal children during the first six to eight years of their schooling. Anyone with a respect for traditional education may find our description absurd. But realism requires that we set ourselves a minimum goal, and primitive as it may seem, survival writing *is* writing and so a partial answer to the question heading this chapter. It may be (though the commission does not think so) that the decline of writing is unarrestable. In that case we should be prepared for a drastic overhaul of the writing curriculum. We should settle for some kind of teaching system whereby a minority of boys and girls is given the chance to advance beyond the survival writing presumed to satisfy the needs of the great majority. While the authors of this book disapprove of such a program and do not care to be responsible for separating the sheep from the goats, it must in all justice be considered.

Competent Writing

Survival writing requires some but not much skill, for it deals hardly at all with expressive combinations of words. It is a specialized form of signaling. But competent writing requires considerable skill, the kind gained from training, drill, exercise, and the retrieval through pen and ink of stored knowledge and memories. It also asks for something beyond skill. It is this "beyond" about which theorists and teachers of composition disagree. First, they are not in agreement that this mysterious element can be taught. Second, they are not of one mind as to what it is. Finally, they differ as to how it should be evaluated.

Because most thoughtful citizens think this unnamed but definitive element can be taught, competent writing, however defined and measured, has been the declared goal of the schools. It is the falling short of the goal that elicits the complaints summarized in Chapter 1.

Reasonably skilled ice skaters should be able to get around the rink at moderate speed, without interfering with others, and without falling down too often. They should know how to start, shift direction, and stop. Finally, they should be able to do these things with enough ease and grace to give themselves the pleasurable sensation that is the purpose of the entire exercise. Skaters who do much less than this can survive on the ice, but we do not call them skillful. If they can do a great deal more than this, they have gone beyond skill into the reaches of art, where they give pleasure not only to themselves but also to spectators.

Ice skating as a skill can be learned by anyone not physically handicapped who wants to learn. Writing as a skill can be learned by anyone not mentally handicapped—again, anyone who really wants to learn. In both cases, the student must obey certain rules and submit to a certain amount of occasionally tedious practice. In both cases the rules are absorbed and gradually forgotten. In both cases the practice, the repetition, becomes less tedious as it is replaced by the satisfaction of mastery.

Elements of Competent Writing

Let us for the moment ignore the "beyond" element that distinguishes competent writing. Let us consider to what degree competent writing is made possible by the use of certain tools working upon raw material. The linguist thinks of this raw material as phonemes, defined in the eighth edition of *Webster's New Collegiate Dictionary* as members "of the set of smallest units of speech that serve to distinguish one utterance from another in a language or dialect."* This unit may be theoretically useful, but no one has ever learned to speak or write well by the study of phonemes. As all babies soon find out, the raw material is words, strung into phrases and short sentences or quasi-sentences. To learn the skill of composition the writer must control a sufficient quantity of raw material—words. "Raw material" is not quite satisfactory as a descriptive term, for vocabulary is not discrete or inert. We do not first accumulate it and then find

---

*By permission. From *Webster's New Collegiate Dictionary* © 1979 by G. & C. Merriam Co., Publishers of the Merriam-Webster Dictionaries.

out what to do with it. Almost from infancy, by a process we do not really understand, we work on these words, rearranging them as we gain more understanding of how they work.

As for enlarging our treasury, the memorizing of word lists and definitions or the assiduous reading of the dictionary probably avails us little. Words come to life in context, for instance in talk. The attentive ear is a good machine for generating vocabulary. Reading is an even better one, especially if the reading is slightly *above* the beginning writer's level. But we should note that competent writing does not depend on an immoderately large vocabulary. Indeed, writing may be handicapped by a vocabulary that is unusual, learned, or modish.

We shape and order the words we know with the help of a variety of tools. At first we use these tools with a mysterious, primitive, almost unconscious skill. Later we learn to use them with greater calculation. Later still we learn that the tools have names. But the names are mere labels, conveniences for study. Some of these writing tools we call penmanship, spelling, capitalization, punctuation, and grammar, which includes syntax. Grammar is named last because it is the only really controversial item on the list and calls for special treatment.

When applied properly to an adequate vocabulary, these basic tools of composition produce an artifact that begins to resemble simple, competent writing. Their use, like the use of hammer and saw, can be taught. The use of more sophisticated devices and techniques, which produce more complex, more competent writing, can also be taught, though with more effort. These we consider later.

Penmanship and Spelling

Except for grammar, there is little to be said about the basic tools, beyond stressing the obvious fact that, whatever writing is, it must reflect their proper use. In a way, the simplest of these tools, penmanship, is the most important. What is *utterly* illegible can be called writing only in a Pickwickian sense. Penmanship is of course not writing; it is a form of drawing, and a case might be made for turning it over to the art teacher. There is no case, however, to be made for teaching an "ideal" handwriting, such as that laboriously achieved by librarians. Minimum legibility is all we have a right to require and all we have time to teach. Furthermore, we can teach only the basic outlines and linkages of the letters. The final *style* of people's handwriting is personal and unique and may indeed, as some say, express the unchangeable essence of their souls.

A word is a design, which, once committed to memory, we can recognize when we meet it again. We do not learn to spell in obedience to any "laws" of correctness. We learn to spell merely because it is more convenient to reidentify the picture we call the word if its form, its outline, is standard and invariable. The imaginative child may draw a cat with one leg, or three, or fifty. But a child who wants the drawn cat to be universally hailed as a cat sticks to four legs. And never mind Picasso.

Underlying the argument based on eye recognition is the fact that anarchic spelling would soon make writing itself difficult, perhaps impossible, and so remove any need for this chapter at all. Again, E. D. Hirsch treats this matter in *The Philosophy of Composition:*

> Despite the defects of the spelling system as it stands, the advantages of any standard system—of any orthography—must, on impartial judgment, far overbalance these defects. For without a normalized, universal way of spelling words in the language, there could be no continuing connection between written and oral speech over all regions where the language is spoken. The alternative to a normalized orthography would be more strictly phonetic spelling, constantly changing in different regions and ultimately creating . . . mutually unintelligible languages. . . . A purely phonetic system of spelling for each region would lead to a babel as great, perhaps, as did the ideographic system in China.[2]

Perfect spelling is *not* essential to competent writing. It is merely desirable. And, to dispose dogmatically of a familiar argument, it would have been desirable in Shakespeare's time also. Even if accompanied by control over the other elements of good writing, marked inability to spell can bring with it a real failure to communicate. We should also note that, whether or not we approve of such artificial status symbols, the poor speller is apt to be suspected, perhaps unjustly, of a more general illiteracy. A correctly spelled but dull letter of application will often secure the job when a livelier one dotted with spelling errors will not. The competent writer therefore should be able to spell well without thought. Writers who can spell perfectly without thought are that much better off.

How does one become a good speller? The answer is not at all clear. There is some mystery about it. Absurd as it may sound— and it sounds absurd indeed—perfect spellers often seem to be born, not made. Highly educated persons who speak and write excellently may be erratic spellers (the late Robert Kennedy, for example). Most of us, experience suggests, learn to spell in three ways: by reading, which through repetition impresses on the eye and therefore the mind and memory the "right" arrangement of letters that form any given word; through various forms of drill familiar to all teachers; and by memorizing whatever rules, not always consistent in our highly evolved language, that may guide us with respect to difficult or unfamiliar words. The writer of these lines, who is lucky enough to be a good speller, calls on his experience in declaring that a proper mix of these three methods will in most cases ensure adequate spelling. But he believes in a very uneven mix: about 75 percent reading, 15 percent earnest drill, 10 percent rule memorizing. Avoid any spelling manual that lists both the correct *and* the incorrect forms. We are just as likely to remember the latter as the former.

two sum up the prakticle cas fer korekt spelin and fer crekt punctueshn too deepens on the advantejiz of won aksepted cod over meny indavidule coads kurect speling savs the tim of both reeder and riter the disadvantaj is the dredfle crool erozn of the childs fredm of egspreshon from wich of corse fu childrn ever ricuvr

Grammar

Mark Twain recommends that writing contain "here and there a touch of good grammar for picturesqueness." We smile sympathetically. Yet we know that, except when he uses bad grammar for effect, Twain's own prose is perfectly "correct." Behind his remark lies the feeling all of us have that the detailed, systematic, and protracted *study* of grammar is certainly boring and probably not very useful. William Cook of our commission has dug up a statement, dated 1873, by Francis Wayland Parker: "The pupils could parse and construe sentences and point out the various parts of speech with great facility, repeating the rules of grammar applicable to each case, yet were unable to put this theoretical knowledge to any practical use, as they showed when called upon to write an ordinary English letter." One hundred and four years later the same view is even more forcibly expressed: "The teaching of grammar has a negligible or, because it usually displaces some instruction and practice in actual composition, even a harmful effect on the improvement of writing."[3]

The present "back-to-basics movement" has at least one built-in weakness: a nervous eagerness on the part of some teachers and parents to assume that because "permissive" education has failed, a wholesale reversion to 1900 will succeed. The evidence does seem to show that old-fashioned parsing and diagramming or new-fashioned transformational grammar, though both give us insight into the structure of the language and are useful in *revising*, probably do not help us greatly in *composing* sentences.

The general attitude of the commission (there was not total agreement) is reflected in the Council for Basic Education *Bulletin* of January 1978. We quote it in full as a sane and moderate view of the relation between grammar and competent writing:

> Our suspicion that the word *grammar* is commonly misunderstood and frequently abused has been pretty well confirmed in the course of our work for the CBE Commission on Writing. Friends who endorse the communication's aims are often quick to suggest that writing skill has gone downhill because "they don't teach grammar very well any more," or to acknowledge their own shortcomings in writing with the explanation that "I've forgotten most of the grammar I learned in school." There seems to be a general assumption among laymen that grammar is the critical mass in learning to write: and if not all teachers share that assumption, many partake of the misunderstanding of the word. Asked what she meant by "language arts," one elementary school teacher replied succinctly, "Grammar."
>
> Whether or not they consider it critical, the mass people have in mind when they use the word *grammar* is usually a

hodgepodge of grammar, syntax, spelling, and punctuation, together with some of the conventions of usage. It is something they learned in school, very likely by drill and by rote, and the experience left them with the impression that learning to write is a dull, difficult business. To the citizen concerned about the condition of student writing, grammar is a necessary evil; to many teachers, it is just evil.

The hodgepodge, of course, is not grammar, and the truth of the matter is that knowledge of grammar—in and of itself—has little to do with the process of writing. Grammar is a language, study or discipline which has to do with the classification of words and their functional relationships in sentences. If the teaching of writing has often been hampered by excessive drill in grammar and by irrelevant excursions into its complications, it has recently been confused by some linguist, and others who are probably more interested in philosophical inquiry into the nature of language than they are in teaching writing to girls and boys in schools. Finding the latinate character of traditional grammar inadequate and not altogether accurate for our language, they developed "structural linguistics"; and when structural linguistics proved wanting, they invented "transformational grammar." Confusion has been compounded by findings of research which tend to show that "instruction in grammar does not contribute to the improvement of student writing." These findings have been joyfully accepted as gospel by teachers for whom grammar has become a dirty word which implies dehumanizing education.

Few teachers gainsay the validity of instruction in spelling or punctuation, although there may be valid differences about methods of instruction. If some flout conventions of usage as "elitist," most subscribe to them. What, then, about grammar? The experience of people who write much, and well, suggests that grammar is seldom, if ever, a function of writing. Writers, that is to say, do not ordinarily approach their writing grammatically. An experienced writer's pronouns tend to fall automatically into agreement with antecedents; and although he may subordinate one statement to another with clear and conscious purpose, he does so without planning to use a subordinate clause. A working knowledge of grammar *is* useful, however, in teaching and learning writing. When one is teaching or learning how to put words together for a purpose—to compose them—it is useful to know what to call them and how they function together. "Working knowledge" implies understanding of course, and many if not all the terms of grammar have perfectly understandable meaning (subordinate, coordinate, active, passive, noun, pronoun, restrictive, non-restrictive, etc.). Such knowledge helps not only to achieve "correctness," but also to develop accuracy and precision of statement, to make emphases and shades of meaning, to develop style.

Perhaps the linguists and grammarians will one day "get it all together" and develop an eclectic grammar which is more comprehensive, adequate, and functional than any of the grammars now available. In the meantime, teachers of writing may safely settle for traditional grammar, if they take to heart these caveats: (1) Grammar is conceptual, and has limited value in teaching very young children. (2) The objective of teaching grammar at any level is working knowledge, not exhaustive knowledge. (3) Grammar is not utterly prescriptive in good writing.

To this statement we might add two comments. The reader might recall in Molière's *Le Bourgeois Gentilhomme* that M. Jourdain is delighted to discover that for more than forty years he has been speaking prose without knowing it. We are all Jourdains. Without any deep study of antecedents or subordinate clauses we speak more or less grammatically. A certain quantity of grammar can be absorbed unconsciously. Reading, whether varied or intensive, helps, as it does with spelling and vocabulary. Another aid is suggested by William Cook in his paper "What Grammar?" prepared for the commission: "There is a difference between grammar taught with an end of systematic mastery of language and grammar taught without application to writing and speaking. If we wish to improve usage, it is more efficient to have students practice composing imitations of desirable forms than to have them memorize rules."

While this counsel is sound, a case can be made for some knowledge, on the student's part, of the *basic* grammatical terms and relations. When students have these basics clearly in mind, they can comprehend more quickly the teacher's criticism of a faulty sentence. But a fair amount of grammar can be taught without relying on diagramming or the memorizing of rules. It would seem useful to drop in a little grammar here and there, as it were, during the process of teaching composition. Beginning with the simpler elements (such as the names and uses of the parts of speech), one can, by connecting such information with actual writing rather than studying grammar as a self-contained discipline, create in the students' mind a growing sense of how language works. Such indirect instruction need not extend to subtleties or exceptional usages. Its range should be limited to the core knowledge that will help to produce competent writing. But, whatever the limitations, it is essential that the students really understand that competent writing is not possible if, for example, subject and verb disagree in number. We believe this understanding can be achieved without recourse to much formal grammatical drill, analysis, or rule memorizing.

Other Elements

Just as competent writing can be achieved by those who are not perfect spellers (though perfection is the aim), so writing that contains occasional errors in punctuation and capitalization can also be judged competent. The conventions governing the use of both these simple tools are neither difficult nor numerous. Nor should we accord them undue reverence. The use of the comma, for example, is a somewhat flexible affair; different writers, though all excellent, may handle it in quite different ways, all equally acceptable. It is not hard to learn what a comma is supposed in general to do, and this function is worth learning. But more important than rules for comma use is the ability to say your sentence in your mind or aloud and realize, "That pause needs a comma," or "If I use a comma here the sentence will be a little clearer."

The effective construction of sentences and paragraphs cannot be learned by rote but only by practice and taking thought. The present writer once learned many years ago that sentences are simple, compound, or complex, or that they are loose, balanced, or periodic, and he has recently learned that they may be "cumulative." It seems unlikely that this knowledge has ever helped him to construct a good sentence, however. What does help a writer to correct faults is self-editing or, when he is lucky, editing by a fresh eye. Reading the sentence aloud often helps, but few of us have the time to read aloud everything we write.

The rules for the construction of paragraphs are also to be viewed with good-natured skepticism. It is not necessary to deify the topic sentence. This paragraph happens to have one, but many sound paragraphs do not. Nor does a topic sentence always lead off. Common sense should guide us as we paragraph, the feeling that our thinking is taking a turn, striking out in a slightly new direction. There are methods for building a paragraph—by comparison, by contrast, by examples, and so forth—but these should not be used mechanically. If we have given thought (not necessarily in detail) to what we want to say and then become interested as we express that thinking in writing, the chances are good that we have unconsciously chosen a method that works.

We have now discussed to what degree competent writing as a skill may be achieved through the proper handling of a few basic tools working on an adequate vocabulary. But that is not enough. We suggested that there is a "beyond," an element somewhat more difficult to define and certainly more difficult to teach—though it does not follow that it is more difficult to *learn*. Without some control over this elusive "beyond," writing falls short of competence.

Idiom, Usage, and "Correctness"

The "beyond" includes idiom and usage, perhaps the soul of a language. It is idiom and usage that distinguish the *feel* of one language from that of others. But they also distinguish the language at any given time from its past and future forms. They distinguish it too from a manufactured language, such as Esperanto, whose rigid structure precludes the shadings, the tone, as well as the growth and evolution, of idiom.

When, in addition to an ability to handle the basic tools, we have an adequate control over idiom and usage, we are on the road to becoming competent writers—granted that we have something to say and know how to put that something together. When our control is more than merely adequate, our writing may advance beyond competence into the domain of excellence. At that point it is more than a skill. It is an expressive art. But "self-expression" or "creativity" is possible only when the student has gained some control over the act of writing. That control involves, among other things, some familiarity with standard, accepted idiom and usage.

There is no point in discussing idiom and usage unless we can agree that there is such a thing as "correctness." Idiom changes: Shakespeare's idiom is not ours. But at any moment, despite minor variations, a norm does exist. This norm is established by good writers and speakers, not forever, but for their particular audience. In other words, if we believe that "mistakes don't matter," that there is no such thing as correctness in language, we are saying in effect that such a norm does not exist or, if it exists, need not be respected.

In a commission paper called "Mistakes in English," Jacques Barzun touches the heart of the matter: "Correctness has nothing to do with snobbery or self-awarded superiority; it has to do with maintaining the integrity of a language." Mr. Barzun's thinking on this matter is worth pursuing more fully:

> To begin with, there are ways of speech that anybody, no matter how ignorant, would at once spot as "not English"; for instance the advice found in a Portuguese-English conversation manual: "Apply you at the study during that you are young." We laugh and say, "The author of that handbook did not know English," even though we understand well enough what he means. The proper English of it is: "Study hard while you are still young."
>
> If that is our spontaneous reaction, the correctness is *in some sense* a recognizable attribute of language. It is not an idea but a fact obvious to all that native speakers of English do not say "during that you are young." This phrasing is *a mistake* for: "while you are young." And a further feeling for idiom suggests that the natural way to express the thought *in English* is to say "while you are *still* young."
>
> So far, so good. But what of the challenge with which students and others defend the linguist's proposition that in a living tongue anything goes, provided some meaning can be glimpsed? These good people say in effect: "Never mind the Portuguese manual; it's a freak. Nobody will ever follow its

absurd example; so its vagaries take care of themselves. But consider the native writers who are good enough to be journalists, public men, scientists, bankers and business men, lawyers and government officials, teachers in schools and universities—why carp at the *supposed* mistakes that they commit, such as using *fortuitous* to mean *fortunate;* scrambling idioms in *cannot help but hope* (instead of *cannot but hope* or *cannot help hoping*); and confusing sound and sense as in: *if I could of, I would of.* Hundreds of similar scrambles are heard and written daily, without apparent damage to public health or the economy. . . . Sensible people go for the meaning. "Effective communication" is the only test.

This argument in favor of a free-for-all in language is a tangle of thought-clichés that must be teased apart, looked at separately, and discarded. "Effective communication" is a meaningless standard. It does not specify the degree or kind of effect. Was not the Portuguese writer, for example, sufficiently effective? He "got his meaning across," though at the cost of making us laugh. Again, suppose that *fortuitous* is used in a sentence where it makes good sense in the meaning *chanceful, accidental,* but we find from a later remark that the writer meant by it *fortunate, lucky:* does our backtracking and self-correction after being mislead leave him an effective writer? The answer takes the form of another question: Is it the writer's business or ours to make his sentences consistent by using the right word? Finally, is the purpose of writing to convey merely the gist of successive meanings or the fullest possible understanding of the idea? "Idea" here includes fact, information, instructions, and thus leaves no doubt as to the answer: unless he is trying to deceive, the user of language has an obligation to prevent misunderstanding at the same time as he informs. . . .

The best English is . . . a fact of experience, not an arbitrary choice. That is best which offers the widest range of expression, in vocabulary, in forms, in devices for distinguishing or uniting related ideas, and which also has by its tradition the best chance of being intelligible to the greatest number, now and hereafter. The linguists themselves call this traditional, albeit changing, language Standard English and their own use of it is a confirmation of its advantages. Its name also implies the reality of "correctness" and the possibility of "mistakes." For "standard" means norm—a criterion of right and wrong—or else there would be no way of telling Standard English from sub-standard. . . .[4]

Standard English, then, true to its name, assumes a standard, and that standard assumes appropriate, though not eternally fixed, idiom and usage. How can we master this important element of competent writing? When learning a foreign tongue we become familiar, through study and rote memory, with lists of idioms. But this method works less well with our own language, even though it may have some modest value for a student who, let us say, is proficient in Black English but uncertain in Standard English. Generally speaking, idiom is best assimilated by listening to people who speak well and by reading the work of people who write well. In the preceding sentence *usually* might have been used instead of *generally.* But *generally* sounded better. In an unpublished paper on the teaching of writing, Carl Bereiter and his associates ask how students can know which of two expressions they have devised is better without already being a skilled writer. "The answer is," they write, "by reference to stored mental models. Therein lies the relevance of reading to writing, a matter in need of extensive investigation."[5]

One wonders how pressing this need for studying the reading-writing link really is. Most educators agree that reading helps writing and that in particular reading nourishes the feeling for idiom. Having investigated the problem, Frank Heys, Jr., writes that the teacher is probably secondary: "The influence of reading on the ability to write appears to be a separate factor, not directly related to the teacher's personality and enthusiasm."[6] The mastery of correct idiom and usage would appear to be largely a do-it-yourself job, except to the extent that the alert teacher recognizes unidiomatic usage in speech and writing and labels it for what it is—a mistake, trivial or serious, depending on the context.

Mechanics, idiom, simplicity, directness, economy: all are hallmarks of competent writing. But at least two other constituents must be noted. The first involves the atoms of composition—words. The second concerns a property of larger structures—form. When we fix our attention on words, the aim is precision. When we fix our attention on larger entities, the aim is organization.

Precision

Whether composing first-grade sentences or college-entrance expository essays, we must have at our disposal an adequate, suitable vocabulary. But to know words, whether few or many, is not quite enough. We must be able to choose among them, to feel that one is better than another. The first-grader may know two words that are somehow connected with pleasant experience. One is *good*, the other is *happy*. Which is better for the thought at hand? The neophyte writer who stops for just a second to reflect before choosing one word over another has already grasped the notion of precision. This student is on the road to competent writing, and furthermore is teachable.

For the professional writer precision in word choice is mandatory, or should be. For the competent writer it is at least a goal to be kept constantly in mind. Writers who do not harbor this goal will incline toward the "just as good," and soon cease to take active advantage of the large passive vocabulary they possess. Mark Twain's often-quoted adage should not intimidate the would-be competent writer; yet its soundness must be acknowledged. "The difference between the right word and the almost right word," wrote Twain, "is the difference between lightning and the lightning-bug."

Another literary reference will help to stress the importance of writing as precisely as possible—as well as the satisfaction therein. In James Barrie's novel *Sentimental Tommy*, Tommy fails to win an essay prize because "the gowk had stuck in the middle of his second page." Why? "For lack of a word. . . . He had wanted a Scotch word that would signify how many people were in church and it was on the tip of his tongue but would come no farther." Says one of the dominies, "Surely the art of essay-writing consists in using the first word that comes and hurrying on." That's what the winner did. But not Tommy (who is of course the boy Barrie). After the examinations, as they are all preparing to leave the school, Tommy suddenly exclaims, "I ken the word now. It came to me a' at once: it is hantle!" And his teacher says to himself, "He *had* to think of it till he got it—and he got it. The laddie is a genius!"[7] In the classroom we are not trying to produce Barries, but this passage makes instructive reading. It dramatizes both the pleasure and the importance of precision.

It is easy enough to counsel precision. But, unless students intuitively recognize how to apply the word to their own mental processes, they may find themselves at a loss. How do professional writers actually go about the business of weighing words and phrases against alternatives? How, concretely, are such decisions made? Is it possible to dramatize the process? We asked Jacques Barzun to write a piece in which, as it were, he thinks out loud for us, demonstrating how a professional writer actually works when the prime aim is clear exposition. Its use to us here lies in the procedure by which the author achieves, after much pencil-chewing, travail, and trial and error, final precision in phrasing and vocabulary. His paper follows.

Thinking, Writing, and Precision
Jacques Barzun

It is a commonplace that the effort to write clearly compels a writer to think accurately. A similar remark often made by writers themselves is that they do not fully know what they think until they have written it down. These maxims conceal two seemingly different activities that interweave in the course of writing. One is the marshalling of one's thoughts— the substance of the essay, letter, opinion, description, or piece of news. The other is the calling forth of just the right words to fit the substance. Unpracticed writers may fail at either task or both. But steady practice takes care of the two difficulties at the same time. For the link between word and thought pulls in both directions: the words—say, those of your title or theme—imply at once by association a number of ideas. Put one down and it drags out others from your mind in a more or less continuous stream—assuming, of course, that you have worked up the facts beforehand. And in reverse, the thought or fact thus dragged out has a shape of its own that demands exact wording. In short, attending by turns to the words on your page and the fragments of sentences in your mind gets the paper written, and it does this in a continuous act of thinking.

Usually, the less strenuous part is to fix and hold the thought flitting through the mind—many different words will capture it. But once two or three such ideas lie side by side, the difficult task begins of making sure that they hang together logically, factually, emotionally, atmospherically, and so on, through all the characteristics that belong to words. Unexpected joinings may bring out clashing elements, the needs of grammar and syntax create confusions, and generally, language which ought to be as fluid as water can be as resistant as granite.

All this wisdom is no doubt true, but it is abstract, and in most discussions of writing it remains so. Others have to take it on faith. Here, for a change, we make it a concrete, direct experience, by showing how the writer's mind worked in the act of writing this and the previous two paragraphs; after which we shall see how another mind failed to pay the same kind of attention in writing a passage that found its way into print. In judging the workings of the mind, remember that they sound both more lumbering and more obvious when they are explained in detail than they are in the act of composition.

The top line of the opening paragraph above read at first: *It is a commonplace remark that to write clearly.* . . . Thinking soon showed that *remark* was unnecessary and *the effort* was needed before *to write* if the meaning was to be conveyed as quickly and clearly as possible. In the sentence, *These maxims* . . . the word first used was *propositions* instead of *maxims.* That word seemed pompous and failed to suggest how often the statements had been used in discussions of writing. Next came: *different elements in the act of writing*, which was flat and dull; it did not show the writer at work as *activities that interweave* does. The original version of the sentence now beginning *For the link between* . . . read: *For the very relation between word and thought pulls.* . . . But does a relation pull? Besides, words ending in *-tion* are generally weak. So *link* was dredged up to consciousness, with the clear gain that links do pull and are vivid things.

In the first sentence of the second paragraph, hesitation occurred over *the less strenuous part is to*—what, exactly? *Clarify?*—no; *seize*—no, *pin down*—and that still wasn't right because two ideas are wanted to show in a flash what happens: *fix* and *hold*. What was to be fixed and held was at first *the fleeting thought*, but when the mind concentrates on writing, it is no vague idea escaping on the fringe of consciousness that one wants to catch, it is one of a pack wriggling in all directions, hence: *The thought flitting through*. Immediately after, there was need of another synonym for *seize*. *Catch* suggested itself, but was ruled out because the colloquial expression *will catch it* raises up the idea of punishment. *Capture* filled the need.

The next sentence on this topic was quickly set down as: "Once these thoughts are seen side by side, it is easy to—*see* naturally came uppermost, but the repetition was downright silly: when something is seen it is easy to see. Yet no other verb filled the meaning—*perceive* or *observe* would be a mere concealment of the unwanted *see*. The idea needed not just a word but a fresh turn of phrase and indeed of thought. The demand produced what you find above about *the difficult task*. . . .

The next and final thought claiming attention was that of doubt, which a listener feels about advice given in hackneyed generalities. To imply this distrust, the opening of paragraph three began: *All this may be true* . . . , but that wording overstated the doubt; it was first changed to *probably true*—still too doubting. Happily there is an English idiom *no doubt*, which says *no, doubt*, and means it, but with a slight reservation—just the phrase wanted to convey the belief of the speaker, coupled with the idea that the reader may still hesitate to believe.

We then come to: *Here, for a change* . . . , which in the first draft was followed by *it should be made a concrete personal experience*. *Should* was sensible but not enough of a promise. If it *should* be done here, it *will* be done, we *make* it so. *Personal experience* was very bad: what other kind of experience is there? And it didn't meet the situation complained of before, that the reader has to take the truth of the maxims on faith. He must be given not personal, but *direct* experience, that is, not at second hand. Another decided change was made in the phrase following, where the jargon *process of composition* stood in first draft: *process* is overused, and besides it should refer to what happens as the product of natural forces—photosynthesis or decomposition. Strike out *process of composition*. Let it be *act of writing*.

Turn now to a short paragraph on which, manifestly, much

less thought has been expended, for it is anything but easy to read or clear when read:

> It may be that in the first year after 1968 the number of minority individuals motivated to apply to medical school and judged qualified for admission was enlarged by the inclusion of a number of somewhat older individuals for whom entry into predominantly white medical schools previously might have seemed hopeless. This backlog may have been largely eliminated over a five- or six-year period, so that fewer such persons would be available for the pool of applicants.

The first sentence is difficult to understand not only because it goes on and on without proper joints to mark places where distinct subjects come into play, but also because the cluster of related facts was never analyzed into groups by the headlong writer. He did not think far enough. For example, the first *number of individuals* was not in fact *enlarged* by some other group *included* later; it was large to begin with, because it consisted of new and leftover applicants. These last had been held back earlier by their feeling that it was hopeless to apply.

Once this knot has been untied the meaning of *backlog* in the next sentence becomes clear: and the *such persons* is then seen to refer to the older, leftover contingent among the applicant group. As for the final clause, it confuses the reader again by the idea of fewer *available*, which suggests short supply of something desired, whereas the idea is this: having been absorbed, this older type of applicant will not recur.

To sum up, this paragraph shows that the person who had studied the facts never sorted out his vague whirling thoughts or disentangled them from other irrelevant thoughts, such as availability. For lack of this isolating of ideas, the words that would have made the links between them clear and exact were never looked for, or found.

Anyone who begins to practice writing discovers, as the reader has noticed here, that composition and revision each set up a steady dialogue within the mind—"Do I mean this?—No, I don't; it says too much (too little) (something else). What then, would do the trick?—Well, perhaps *seize*.—No, too strong (or:

repeats)—What about *catch, fix, hold, capture?*—Choose one, and try it—Yes, that's it!"

The habit of question and answer for this purpose carries over into speech: the writer doesn't fumble quite so much as before he began to write, and soon his better spoken expression aids him in his writing. If suddenly called on for a statement, oral or written, he is less likely than a nonwriter to fall into incomprehensible jargon or to say the opposite of what he means—as we see our leaders in all walks of life doing every day in the newspapers. A typical instance will round out this little exposition of the thought-and-word interdependence, which so easily turns into a misconnection. After a serious power failure and blackout in a large city of the Southwest, the spokesman for the stricken electric company told the press, "Hopefully we can wait another thirty or forty years for something like this to happen again. Of course we can't guarantee it will take that long either." In other words, "We should wait patiently for our hope of another blackout to come true. But don't be cast down, it may well come sooner than I've led you to think."

So ends Mr. Barzun's illustration of the way the writers' minds work when they are anxious to achieve precision in words and phrases.

We now consider thinking in a broader sense, as having to do with the ordering of one's thoughts. In passing, we might note that Mr. Barzun's entire paper is a model of the sort of thinking that results in well-organized writing.

Thinking and Organization

We return to E. D. Hirsch to start our thinking about thinking:

> Highly logical and clear-headed students often write badly because they fail to make explicit some of the implicit logical connections in their argument. But even when they make such connections, they may still write badly. There is, in fact, a logical flaw in equating clear thinking and clear writing. The word *clear* means something different in the two phrases. Clear thinking means drawing correct inferences from the given premises. Clear writing means an

unambiguous and readable expression of one's meaning. I have argued, and have illustrated the point, that muddy writing can express clear thinking and that clear writing can express muddy thinking.[8]

Mr. Hirsch's point that clear thinking does not *automatically* equal clear writing is sound. We often feel that in our heads there dwells a clear idea but that we "just can't find the right words for it." We have all read prose in which clear ideas were laid out one after another like sticks of wood—and yet the passage, though penetrable, made unattractive reading and so communicated poorly. The writer had perhaps chosen too many rough equivalents of the ideal precise words and phrases, or omitted connectives, or used a series of brief, monotonous declarative statements, or reemphasized the clear ideas to the point of tedium. Such small rhetorical crimes are innumerable, and any of them can interfere with clarity of expression.

As we turn to examine the kinds of thinking that result in well-organized writing we concern ourselves with the shape and design of the whole piece rather than of sentences. But it is well to remember that the whole is the sum of its parts. For the whole to be excellent, its parts must be carefully constructed.

You will recall Barrie's heroic Tommy. Because he was in love with precision his dominie hailed him as a genius. The judgment was premature. Unless Tommy had also been capable of organizing the precise words he so conscientiously sought into a well-wrought whole he would not have become a writer.

It is difficult to teach form. By their very nature formally excellent structures do not call attention to themselves, and so are not greatly useful as models. All one can say is that competent writing, whether narrative or expository, whether a paragraph, a research paper, a letter, or an essay, must have a shape, no matter how simple. A narrative has a beginning, a middle, and an end. A paragraph should develop one idea and then stop; or, if it develops several ideas, it should be so constructed as to emphasize the more important and subordinate the less. If there are several paragraphs, one should lead to the other, though not always through the use of connectives.

Before we start to write a paragraph or longer composition all we can do is ask ourselves a few simple questions. Do I really *have* an idea or am I just putting down some words in the hope that they will suggest an idea, and so, by a series of happy accidental associations, generate a composition? Can I phrase my idea very roughly in my head before I put it down in words? Is it an idea so complex that it needs to be broken down into parts? If not, can it be handled in a single paragraph? Do I have some sense, precise or vague, of another and connected idea with which to follow it? If I am pretty certain that I have quite a few notions rattling about in my head, why not set them down in the briefest possible form, look them over, and decide (a) which notion is the most important, requiring the most development; (b) which is a good one to lead off with; (c) which is a good one to finish with; and (d) whether a final summary is necessary or useful. Note that such a sketchy listing of ideas need not involve a formal outline with many subdivisions. An elaborate outline is rarely required for most school work and may hobble rather than order one's thoughts. A frame is not a straitjacket.

We have so far been talking about prose that is mainly expository or descriptive or argumentative. But preliminary thinking is just as necessary when we propose to write narrative (let us say an account of a personal experience), though the questions we ask ourselves are a little different. Do I remember my experience in sufficient detail to make possible a composition of the desired length? Why am I telling this story—that is, how do I wish to affect my reader? I must have a beginning, but is it best to tell my tale in strict chronological order, or begin with my most vivid recollection, or perhaps even start by hinting at the climax and then reverting to the opening episodes? If I have a climax, or an important turning point, what is it? Does my story gain by direct, lean narration, in Hemingway's manner, or does it require touches of color—description, even personal running comment?

We stress here the banal details of what used to be called unity and coherence (perhaps they still are) because during the past few decades these elements of composition have been scorned by a part of the educational avant-garde, who have concentrated on what they see as the students' need above all to "do their own thing." But depending on inspiration and the creative impulse alone reduces one's chances of producing competent writing. The self-expressive urge and the structural urge do not run easily in tandem—and it is the former that in some quarters has been given the preference. Children playing with building blocks might *like* to express their fantasies by building a tower with a one-block base and a multiblock superstructure. They soon discover that it cannot be done: the tower collapses. They must sacrifice their desires to the requirements of the laws of physics. By satisfying those requirements they can experience a different pleasure, which comes of obeying reason rather than indulging in dreams.

In considering this distinction we have slipped into the realm of "creative writing." Perhaps this term, along with the word *creativity* itself, should be banned from polite language. A superintendent of schools in a California city recently left his post to take a job developing schools in Saudi Arabia. "It's a fantastic opportunity," he said, "especially from the point of creativity." There is no doubt about what he meant: it's interesting to develop a school system. But, first, by using the cheap language of Hollywood (*fantastic*); second, by the unconscious murder of idiom (*from the point of creativity*); but especially by using *creativity*, a word that resists definition, he makes us a trifle anxious about the educational future of the little Saudi Arabians.

In certain quarters the cult of "creative writing" is a pretext for avoiding the labor of organizing one's writing. A. Bartlett Giamatti, who taught English and comparative literature at Yale before becoming its president, writes,

> High school and college students have been encouraged to believe that language does not require work—that if they wait they will suddenly blossom and flower in verbal mastery; that if they transcribe what they feel about anything it will somehow turn into what they think. Clearly, to have been told all those things—and millions of school children were and are told these things—is to have been lied to.[9]

When young students are told to put down what comes into their heads or to write a poem and not to worry about the rules, and are consequently congratulated on being creative writers, they are, as Giamatti says, being lied to. Any good piece of writing, even when it is a piece of free association—for example, Molly Bloom's monologue in *Ulysses*—has a calculated shape. Charles Lamb's *Dream Children* is as carefully composed as real dreams and reveries are incoherent.

Children or teenagers who feel an impulse to set down on paper elements of their "inner life," random thoughts and confusions, resentments and obsessions, should by all means do so—in a private diary. (Arn and Charlene Tibbetts report that one English teacher calls this the "who-I-am-and-why-I-hate-my-mother syndrome."[10]) As an assigned composition such perfectly natural exercises in narcissism are not acceptable, and children performing them should not be told that they have "created" anything. Doubtless the motive behind the injunction to write creatively contains an element of benevolence, the desire to "liberate" the student. But the self, as Mr. Barzun might say, "can't be found like a lost umbrella." Direct liberation is not the English teacher's business even though the proper study of literature and composition may be, indeed is, indirectly liberating. A composition should not be a medium of mental or emotional therapy, any more than is the learning of plane geometry. Writing may have certain side effects on the personality, for no student can construct a good (or bad) paragraph without gaining insight, even if it be only a sense of dissatisfaction, into the content of his own mind. But writing may do more; it may enlarge that content. Henry Adams tells us, "The habit of expression leads to the search for something to express."

Learning to write competently is true self-education, not therapy, or the self-indulgence masked by that word. It was Montaigne who said, "I have no more made my book than my book has made me." While it is not true that *merely* writing (in whatever quantity) will teach one to write, it is true that writing, when constrained by a constant search for precision and a constant concern for form, can help one to write better and to become a more organized human being.

These constraints are weakened when students are over-encouraged to think of self-expression as an end in itself, or to cut up loose and incoherent prose into short lengths and label it poetry. In the latter instance the damage is doubled. Not only do students thereby produce incompetent writing, but they remain permanently unsure as to what properly distinguishes genuine writing from the likes of their own outpourings. It is possible that undisciplined "free" writing may be useful as a warm-up exercise. But we believe that such an exercise has little more usefulness than that.

The unbridled "creative writing" that we have been discussing is a form of soliloquy, of self-communication. But our aim is to produce two-way communication. Therefore, students will be helped if they have in mind a specific audience. That audience will differ in accordance with the nature of the assignment. It might be an audience of the writer's peers. It might be, if the assignment were a job-application letter, a presumed employer. The only audience for whom it is risky to write is the teacher. Here the relationship is flawed, because the student is trying to write clearly but at the same time aiming to please the instructor—that is to say, to get a good grade. Obviously we cannot be draconian here—the teacher is bound to be somewhere in the back of the student's mind. It is when such a consideration comes first that we get composition that may be correct but often little beyond that. Therefore, developing a sense of audience is part of the process of learning to write, and one that good teachers keep clearly in mind.

One final point, stressed by Carl Bereiter and his coworkers in their writing-pedagogy study: expository writing usually contains a quantity of facts; merely listing these facts, even in some logical order, or summarizing them, does not produce organized writing. What does lead to organization is the preconceived point or purpose of offering the array of facts. This is what we mean when we speak of the argument (meaning something more than the writer's persuasiveness) of a prose piece. The argument is the armature that underlies and sustains the final shape or form. That armature does not have to be constructed in detail or completely thought out in advance. But it has to be conceived, however approximately, in the mind.

The reader must not infer from the foregoing that we are advocating Gradgrindism. There is a place for creative writing, for narrative, for purely imaginative exercises, for fantasy. We suggest only that all these kinds of writing be guided by some reflection and adherence to a preconceived design and not be the product of free-form associational reverie. Certain students will learn more from creative-writing activities that involve a modicum of intellectual rigor. And grown-ups often find in such efforts a fruitful and important mode of recreation, in the literal sense of the word.

Superior Writing

Effective communication demands more than getting the meaning across. It means getting it across idiomatically and unequivocally. It also means getting it across economically. Communication, argues Mr. Barzun, is most complete when it proceeds from the smallest number of words—and indeed of syllables. The criterion here is similar to that governing a machine—efficiency. As E. D. Hirsch puts it, "A text is said to be more efficient than another if it requires less effort by the reader in understanding the very same meaning."[11]

Of course, many degrees of competent writing exist, some of a very high order indeed. Similarly there are many degrees and kinds of superior writing. Let us take a superlative example of superior writing. "Bare ruin'd choirs, where late the sweet birds sang," makes an efficient statement about the appearance of woods in late fall or winter. It obeys Barzun's rule of verbal and indeed syllabic economy—eight monosyllables, one disyllable. But at once we feel that the line offers more than the efficiency of merely competent writing. It works upon our minds in some way that competent writing does not. We say of such writing that it is superior. Its superiority derives not only from its clarity of expression, but also from the emotions it excites in us, of which admiration is one. Competent writing does not generally excite such emotions.

Our response to this line from Shakespeare's Sonnet 73 is immediate. But on reflection we become aware that the immediacy of our response has been achieved through Shakespeare's use of a number of devices, cunningly combined and partly concealed. These devices are not among those we discussed in connection with competent writing. They are, we say, more sophisticated. One is rhythm, a tool just as applicable to prose, of course, as to verse, though the methods of using it differ. Another is the use of a figure of speech*—in this case the metaphor that likens nature's

---

*It is probable that the traditional, earnest study of "figures of speech" is a waste of classroom time. The teacher should, in the course of the study of literature, casually point them out here and there, just as casually mention their names, and have the student try to identify the work they do in a particular context. It is quite *natural* for us to use figures of speech; what is unnatural is to study them systematically out of their contexts.

architecture, the boughs of a tree, to human architecture, a part of a church, a metaphor intensified by the fact that singing is associated with both forms. Another device is euphony, or the beauty of sound. Another is the skillful repetition of a single consonant, *r*, to give a kind of reverberant, echoing effect. Still another is the contrast between the adjective *sweet* and the adjectives *bare* and *ruin'd*. All these devices belong to what, hardly knowing what we mean but knowing we mean something, what we call creative imagination. An individual creative imagination, working with the same words that anyone might use (the nine words in Shakespeare's line are all familiar ones) produces a communication that has, as we say, style.

Teachers of composition can call attention to models that exhibit style, as we have just tried to do. They can urge the student to study such models. They might, perhaps, suggest composition subjects more likely than others to call forth the imagination of the student. But that is probably all teachers can do to elicit superior writing. Such writing can be encouraged, and if a student is blessed by nature with the imaginative faculty, that faculty can be identified, guided, and developed. But it cannot in any important sense be taught. The best writing should be our aim, but competent writing, which *can* be taught, is what most of us must settle for: *Only a few months ago these bare boughs were full of singing birds.*

The query that heads this chapter cannot of course be answered in the space at our disposal. We have tried only to separate the two ideas of talking and writing, and to distinguish three orders of composition—survival writing; competent writing, which is the achievement goal; and superior writing. In our discussion of competent writing we considered the basic mechanics of the art, the control of idiom and usage, the precise use of words, and the organization of a piece of work. Integral to all these elements is thinking; the art of writing develops out of reflection in advance and reflection after the first draft is completed. What we have tried to do, in effect, is to identify the major components, which when harmoniously combined, result in clear and economical communication.

Chapter 5

The Conditions of Learning

"Expression is the need of my soul," said archy in the first message that literate cockroach left in his boss's typewriter. And so he wrote. Night after night, he "cast himself with all his force upon a key, head downward, and his weight and the impact of the blow were just sufficient to operate the machine, one slow letter after another."[1] Most souls have the same need as archy's but lack his determination. In the age of telecommunications and abundant life not even electric typewriters give souls much incentive to write, and learning to write looks dull and difficult.

Actually, almost anyone of ordinary intelligence can learn to write, and learning does not have to be dull. But learning is conditional. One must have incentive; he must know or feel that he can fill some important need by writing, that he can accomplish a purpose, whether it be to express his soul or simply to pass information along. If he has "an ear for language," he will have an advantage in learning, for those who are accustomed to the sound of language that is well spoken or well read take more naturally to writing than others. And he must also have the encouragement of mentors who understand writing well enough to help him find and make his own way.

There is a popular misconception that writing is a kind of automatic function, that all it takes is a few "basic skills," which can (or should) be learned and mastered in short order, once and for all. Now it may be possible to learn to spell a word in almost no time, and it shouldn't take long to grasp the idea that pronouns are expected to agree with their antecedents; but learning to choose words with accuracy, to put them together in intelligible statements, and then to compose the statements in such a way as to accomplish a purpose—this takes longer.

In the jargon of pedagogy, learning to write is a developmental process, which means simply that no one can learn more than the development of his mind and body enables him to learn at any given stage. It would be foolish, obviously, to expect a sixth-grader to write a paper on economic imperialism even if he knew the basics of grammar, spelling, and punctuation cold. By the same token it would be unwise to ask a twelfth-grader to write the proposal for a foundation grant, even though he might write a fairly respectable paper on economic imperialism. Moreover, at any stage of development, a writer gains proficiency only as he assimilates what he hears, reads, observes, thinks, and does from day to day—and as he writes and rewrites. He progresses and regresses, but only as he gains experience can he gain competence.

At the risk of redundancy, it is worth emphasizing that learning the mechanics of writing is not the same thing as learning to write. Grammar, spelling, punctuation, paragraphing, and the conventions of usage are important, and competent writing requires their knowledge and use. But they are tools of the trade, not the trade itself. Undoubtedly some teachers' relentless drilling in mechanics has contributed to the indelible impression of hosts of sensible people that learning to write is difficult, dull business. More's the pity.

Our purpose in this chapter is neither to expound a theory of learning nor to pass judgment on parents, teachers, or schools for shortcomings or failures that may be theirs. We intend nothing more than to describe some of the conditions that foster the development of a young person's ability to write. Our description is drawn from experience, observation, and discussion. If, along the way, we mention conditions that hinder development, we do so only for the sake of explanation or contrast.

Beginnings

If learning to write is developmental, how, when, and where does the development begin? Ordinarily, it begins at home. Children first learn language by hearing speech in their homes, and it follows that their ability to use the language—to speak it, think it, listen to it, read it, and write it—is profoundly affected by the conditions in which they begin life and spend their preschool years. Home conditions vary: some homes favor the development of language proficiency, some limit or even prevent it.

Home environments cannot be appraised in the simple terms of affluence or poverty. In some wealthy homes conditions may retard learning, and in some poor homes the incentive to learn is strong.

But rich or poor, homes where conditions are not favorable put children from the beginning at a serious disadvantage—one that they take with them to school when the time comes. A legion of devils is at work today undermining American homes, rural, suburban, and inner city; and conflict, poverty, and disease cannot be dismissed as exclusively economic and social ills. Because they have immediate and lasting effect on learning, these ills pose complicated educational problems that cry for solution. It is probably safe to say, nevertheless, that most American homes *can* provide conditions conducive to literacy. Those conditions are our concern here.

Common sense and an awareness of the possible must inform our expectations for American homes, especially those in which there are young children. Parents are busy people and have other things to do than provide an ideal environment for their children's learning. Typically, a young father is among the lower men on some employer's totem pole. He works long hours to earn his pay and to get ahead. As often as not, mother is working too. Both belong to a generation of consumers who are losing the ability to wait for the things that will support the lifestyle to which they hope to become accustomed. Even the most sensible and conscientious would not, and probably could not if they would, give undivided attention to their children's incipient needs for literacy. At the same time, parents who neglect those needs are less than sensible and conscientious. The comforting truth is that providing an environment conducive to literacy does not take undivided attention or endless hours. It takes awareness, concern, and interest (which are not always ready or readily aroused); it takes some effort (which parents, understandably, are sometimes too tired to make); but it takes only incidental time.

So what's a mother to do? And a father? First of all, make a habit of speaking carefully. If the language children first learn is the speech they hear at home, and if they hear parents who speak with care, they will imitate them and store away patterns that will help when they begin to read and write. Not that every father has to sound like Laurence Olivier, or every mother like Katharine

Hepburn. However, by taking a little thought, all parents can avoid the "likes" and "y'knows," the noises and grunts, that have come to make the American tongue infectiously sloppy. Even a parent who don't speak good can speak bad carefully, and those who feel constrained to "speak roughly to their little boy and beat him when he sneezes" don't have to be sloppy about it.

Speaking *to* children is important, and so is conversing *with* them. Physicists with Ph.D.'s may feel awkward trying to engage small children in meaningful discourse, but parents who do precisely that give their youngsters a real advantage. However inane it may seem to the physicists, the discourse means a great deal to the children, who need to ask questions and make statements. Conference, Bacon says, maketh a ready man, and conversation helps to make children ready for writing. (Bacon also says that writing maketh an exact man.) Adults' talking with children—about what they do during the day, what is read to them, what they watch on television—gives children experience in putting words together. Grown-ups can constructively help or prompt them to make clear statements, but they had better not oblige children to speak with adult correctness. They can, and, to the best of their ability, they should, dependably supply young conversationalists with *models* of correctness; but insisting on correctness can effectually distract children from using their minds to do what is most important in conversation—that is, from sorting out ideas and giving the listener the necessary details. Interrupting a child in midtelling to warn against a *who* instead of *whom* is seldom worth the cost of the correction!

If they are going to become literate, children need to make their own statements, and to make these as clear as possible. Conversation enables them to confirm impressions, formulate ideas, control information, and so gives them confidence in using language. Conversation is fundamental to the experience that makes for competence in writing, and parents (not to mention grandparents, siblings, and sitters) who *really talk with* the smaller members of the family help to start them on the way.

Reading aloud does more than provide subjects for conversation. Such reading often kindles young listeners' imaginations almost magically, and it can give them an affection for particular words or—happiest of all—words in general. Better even than good conversation, reading aloud may instill feeling for the way words fit and work together, which is of transcending importance in good writing. It is a boon that reading aloud to children is still a custom in many homes—and a bane that the pace of living so curtails it. Even a few minutes' reading once or twice a week is better than no reading at all, and more than that is better still.

Of course, what one reads aloud and how one reads it makes a difference. Quality is always preferable to quantity. Stories and verse that are well written and well read have the greatest potential benefit; and if few adults qualify as gifted readers, many are at least adequate, and most improve with performance. What matters most is the selection of material. Parents are likely to turn first to what they remember enjoying when they were children—*When We Were Very Young*, perhaps, or *Winnie the Pooh*, *The Wind in the Willows*, *Charlotte's Web*, *Ferdinand the Bull*. It is well to admit, however, that not all the revered classics on which their parents were brought up are liked or understood by children today. Children bored by *Alice in Wonderland* are not necessarily insensitive, unimaginative, or unintelligent. They are simply living in a world just a little too far away from Lewis Carroll's. Some parents read whatever comes to hand, and others turn to the offerings of librarians and booksellers. The production of literature—or rather reading matter—for children is big business, and the quality is considerably less than dependable. Responsible readers-aloud are guided by their own tastes and values, and prescription is a risky undertaking. Notwithstanding, we have appended suggestions on pages 156–160, because nothing can take the place of good reading aloud in developing the ear for language that will help beginners take to writing.

The admission that television fare can be discussed by and with children does not at this point warrant explication of the merits and demerits of the "vast new presence," which is discussed in Chapter 2. The presence is here to stay, and the vast majority of children live within it. "It is a fact," says Dorothy Cohen, "that television viewing starts early in babyhood and goes on forever after."[2] And it is accepted as fact that the influence of television on children's learning is immeasurable, if not immeasurably bad. Our concern here is with whether television makes any contribution to a child's ability to write, and we conclude regretfully that the contribution is at best small. Insofar as television provides inferior language models and anesthetizes imagination, it may be actually destructive of the aptitude for writing. The judgment of David Mackay and Joseph Simp speaks directly to the matter:

> A child left on his own in front of a television set will not gain much experience or learning. In extreme cases too much solitary viewing may help to keep his mind blank by offering him a constant flow of images to consume passively on his own. If television as it is actually offered to the consumer could do linguistic "miracles"—which it cannot—many educational problems would already have been solved.[3]

Assuredly, television does not do linguistic miracles, but it is here to stay and, for better or worse, to teach. Parents who do not depend on television as pacifier or baby sitter, but who with some discrimination choose the programs their children will watch, can sometimes make television a fair teacher. "Sesame Street" has lasted for years even though it does not sell breakfast food because it is a good program. It actually helps preschoolers learn their letters and numbers, and if Frog talks with the breezy banality of newscasters when he's at the scene reporting Humpty Dumpty's fall, he at least speaks with the tongue of a well-trained actor. "Mister Rogers," all by himself, can make such convincing conversation about the spyglass in his hand that a three-year-old boy will focus the lens in the glass he pretends to have in his own hand. Programs are to be found, on public and on network television, that do something for the beginnings of reading and writing, but prolonged immersion in this medium is not recommended.

Simple word games and riddles delight the very young and give them interest in, and familiarity with, words. Robert Gundlach, whose research in children's writing is further discussed below, urges parents to *support* the small child's writing. Accept and admire those first scribbles. Pin them to the bulletin board (a minor but pleasant domestic teaching device) or refrigerator door. The more parents immerse their young children in language, the brighter are children's prospects of learning to write with confidence and skill. The day may come when early childhood education (school for preschoolers) lends effective support, but literacy begins at home.

The Young Child as Writer

Those who despair of the deplorable condition of student writing may contemplate hopefully the fact that elementary school children don't jump to the conclusion that it is too late to learn. As a matter of fact, they are usually eager to learn to write. Donald Graves says, "Children want to write before they read. They are more fascinated with their own marks than with the marks of others. Young children leave their messages on refrigerators, bathroom walls, moist window panes, sidewalks, their bedroom doors, and scraps of paper."[4]

From time to time and place to place, prodigies may appear who can write before they reach kindergarten. Most preschool children, however, simply do not yet have the psychomotor development to write words and sentences, and zealous adults can do more harm than good by pushing them. It is enough for most young children that they be given some sense of the importance and the possible pleasures of writing—first, as a rule, by responding to the strong, apparently natural desire most of them have to draw. Drawing seems to meet a need children have to extend themselves, to reach out into the world around them. When drawing, children often have the same happily absorbed look they exhibit when they first master reading. Parents can help not only by giving them paper and crayons and pencils, but by watching and making suggestions, by encouraging and approving. And it does no harm for them to see their parents writing letters. Suppose father is writing to his own mother, and small daughter, at loose ends, is being a nuisance. Father might say, "I'm writing a letter to grandma. Go watch television." Or, better, he might say, "I'm writing a letter to grandma. How about making a picture for me to send with it?" When the picture is done, he might add, "How about dictating a good title for me to print under the picture?" There is no harm, either, in letting a small child know that mother is writing a very important report and mustn't be disturbed.

The alternatives may seldom be so simple or the options so clear, and parents have to improvise. Improvisation calls for imagination, but not more than most parents have. Anyone can make up a short, short story, and story-telling has an intimate, just-for-you quality. Children love to make up stories themselves, especially if grown-ups will write them down and read them back.

Many children can already recite the alphabet and count to ten or higher when they enter kindergarten, and some can read and print their letters and numbers. Even those not actually eager to learn have not yet built up resistance, and therefore what happens in the primary grades is critical. When principals and teachers recognize the value of writing and have a measure of imagination and common sense about teaching it, the chances are that the cause of literacy will be greatly advanced.

And that may well be happening under our eyes. Popular interest in getting education "back to basics" has badgered some into doing more about the three Rs, but there are those who have always done well. A veteran schoolteacher in Maine has little patience with new-fangled notions of "competency-based education" and thinks the schools have no business teaching students how to iron shirts or use marine instruments. "Basically, Mainers are old-fashioned," Dorothy Wilson says concisely. "We want our children to be able to read, write, and figure." She includes in this knowledge the ability to express thoughts in speech and writing. Further she expects them "to have learned the uses of reading: for information, for pleasure, for following directions," and for finding the facts that "the schools expect them to know."[5]

Three years ago, the principal and teachers of Samuel Greeley School, an elementary school in Winnetka, Illinois, wanted to do more about writing. Through a teachers' center they made connections with a professor at Northwestern University, Robert Gundlach, mentioned earlier, who has made children's writing his special interest. Teachers and professor met from time to time, during the lunch hour or after school, and before long they embarked together on a project. At this writing they have been following the progress of the writing of individual boys and girls for three years, gathering notes on promising teaching practices, collecting data for research, and assembling readings on the subject. The professor's research is increasingly informed by the most reliable kind of data, while the teachers are becoming masters of the art of teaching writing to beginners.

Children in the Samuel Greeley School program are learning to write under conditions that are probably as close to optimum as possible in a school, but other schools foster good conditions as well. For instance, the principal of the Charles Ashley School in New Bedford, Massachusetts, stressed the three Rs in her plans for 1977-1978. She asked teachers to list student learning priorities in language and to make note of those teaching materials they found most valuable. She also wished to discover student weaknesses, review creative* writing assignments, and determine student standings on the most recent language achievement tests. Armed with this information, she hoped to forge a curriculum that addressed student weaknesses; it is not surprising that the curriculum stressed grammar, spelling, dictation, and the writing of stories, letters, and book reports.

The subject known as "English" in the upper grades is commonly called "language arts" in elementary school, and the term may have more meaning than much education jargon has. It comprehends the use of language in listening, speaking, reading, and writing. When the subject is well taught, none of these "arts" strays far from the others. We have touched on the value of speaking and conversing in preschool experience, and these functions—together, of course, with listening—become perhaps even more vital in the comparatively formal learning situation of elementary school. Again, it is generally appreciated that what children read and hear others read influences the development of their skills as writers. It is not so generally understood that writing helps a child learn to read, but that is evidently true as well. Learning to form letters, write words, and put words together into phrases and sentences sometimes begins to solve for beginners the puzzle of reading. Good teachers of the language arts know this, and take advantage of it.

Reading and personal experience (real or imagined) are main sources of the writing children do. With Halloween in sight, for

---

*As one of the language arts taught in the elementary schools, "creative writing" apparently means anything children make up—anything, that is, they do not copy from a book or an encyclopedia, for example. It may be a story, a book report, what have you.

example, a teacher reads a story about goblins to twenty or more third-graders sitting on the floor around her chair. Reading time, say, ten minutes. For the next ten minutes, the class has a conversation about goblins: What *are* goblins? What do they look like? Where do you find them? What would you do if you met a goblin or if you *were* a goblin? Out of the mouths and minds of these third-graders—prompted sometimes by each other, sometimes by their teacher—come answers, experiences, imaginings; and when conversation is full but not yet finished, the teacher dispatches them to their work places. There they go straight to work to create their own goblins, with crayons or water colors. In another day or two, when their pictures and paintings are ready, they will get on with the ultimate task—writing a story to go with the picture, which will take more days. The finished stories may not be very long—a few sentences, perhaps, or a paragraph—but they will be, literally, compositions.

Some kindergarten and first-grade teachers use the device of reverse dictation. The child, not yet a writer, tells a story to the teacher, who writes it down, then hands it back, and—O, miracle!—there it is, the child's own story, preserved, fixed forever, repeatable, show-offable. This little ploy often carries the seed of writing motivation.

In kindergarten and first and second grades, virtually all writing effort is spent on forming letters, words, and a few sentences. Children in fourth, fifth, and sixth grades are doing more and more of their own reading, and they are writing more substantial stories. They are also writing different kinds of compositions—letters, book reports, articles for school newspapers, even research papers of a kind. Letter-writing is very much alive in some classrooms. One teacher has an arrangement with a friend who teaches in another town whereby their students exchange letters. A sixth-grade teacher in Massachusetts has an elaborate project with a teacher in Texas. The teachers write to each other, and their students exchange work done in class (murals, for example, of whaling out of New Bedford for pictures of cowpunching in Texas). Book reports have fallen from grace in the high school, but continue to enjoy the blessing of elementary teachers and the consent of their pupils. For his first book report of his fifth-grade year, this is what one boy wrote about *Charlotte's Web:*

How would you feel if your father were going to take an axe and kill a baby pig? That is exactly what Fern's father was about to do until Fern stopped him. During the spring she played, fed, and helped the baby pig she named Wilbur to drink milk. Wilbur had a friend. It was a spider named Charlotte A. Cavatica. As the years passed by Wilbur was sent to a fair. There he won first prize, and the day after Charlotte died. She left an egg sac which Wilbur took good care of until spring. Some of the story is sad and some is happy.

It would be interesting to know how many elementary schools publish student newspapers. The Samuel Greeley School in Winnetka is one of them, and *The Greeley Snooper* is composed, illustrated, and dittoed by two fourth-grade editors and their staff of ten. A sample issue includes four articles (50 to 150 words), a recipe, a quiz, and an original crossword puzzle. The article that follows appeared in one issue of *The Snooper*. It is the joint effort of a fourth-grader, Dan, and a third-grader, Jordy. Helen Danforth, their teacher, explains, "Although supposedly partners, each boy worked alone on the rough draft. When I insisted that *they* cooperate instead of my choosing between them, they agreed on an amalgamated beginning, and then Dan made the fair copy of Jody's part, and vice versa. I gave them some help, not much, and they labored mightily." Here is the result.

Thanksgiving

Today you're free. But did you know that in England many years ago people had to obey the King's church? Some people wanted to have their own separate church. These people were called Separatists. Separatists had secret meetings. But the king found out about the meetings. Separatists were afraid to stay in England so they went to Holland in 1608. In Holland they found a man from England to get them a ship. This ship was called the Mayflower.

Some people died on the journey. But only about 15 died on the ship. The Mayflower landed at Plymouth Rock on Dec. 21, 1620. The winter that came was so bad only about half the original people survived. Fortunately next summers' harvest was so good they would have food for weeks, so they decided to have a feast. The Indians gave five deer to the feast and ninety of the Indians came! And they called this giant feast THANKSGIVING! And that's how Thanksgiving began.

Inevitably, young writers make mistakes, lots of them, but freedom to make mistakes is a most important condition of learning to write. Ordinary mortals may not understand that, and adults are often too zealous, if not insufferable, about correcting children. Good teachers, on the other hand, know how to evaluate mistakes and can tell when mistakes are "evidence of learning-in-progress," to borrow Robert Gundlach's phrase. Misspelling is perhaps the most conspicuous mistake children make, and when parents see *lade* for *lady*, or *owes* for *always*, they may fear that they have a budding illiterate in the family. Gundlach would tell them that there are common patterns in younger children's "invented spellings" and suggest that misspelling of this kind is a natural feature of most children's written language development. He cites the following example, which might be tagged an advanced case of error in mechanics by those who did not know better.

About five years ago when I was walking home from kindergarten with my mother I asked her if we could get a cat she said no I said could we look at them she said Ok. So we went to some peoples house down the block and asked if they had any cats left.

"Here the lack of punctuation obscures what is actually a rather mature and effective rendering of the boy's conversation with his mother," Gundlach explains. "We need to recognize that this young writer has produced a relatively sophisticated passage." His evaluation is straight to the point: "This fourth grader may be ready to work on the techniques of punctuating dialogue."[6]

Under good conditions, a teacher would seize the moment to teach that fourth-grader to punctuate dialogue, not penalize him for failing to apply rules he may have been given before. This does not imply that good learning conditions are exclusive of correction. Children's mistakes in grammar, punctuation, capitalization, spelling, word usage, and sentence construction need to be corrected, and good teachers make corrections, commonly setting a student to rewrite a composition. Editing, which is an essential part of good writing, is "a difficult cognitive task" even for adults, Gundlach points out, and "younger children are not developmentally ready for this sort of task. It may not be until a child reaches fourth or fifth grade that he is able to understand that editing means more than 'copying over in ink.' "

Nor do the good conditions we are enumerating here necessarily exclude some of the disciplines traditionally associated with learning to write. For example, grammar exercise and spelling drill are helpful; and although both are easily overdone, neither is to be despised. The suggestion sometimes advanced that teachers "treat grammar as you would a cancer: cut it out of the curriculum" is too drastic. Children learn how to put words together more readily when they know what to call them, and sometimes an old-fashioned drill or a spelling bee can be an excellent way to learn what words are and how they are spelled. Constructive and helpful use of any method or technique is always a function of imagination and common sense. Helen Danforth, the Winnetka teacher who is so amply endowed with both, uses drill for the systematic study and mastery of word families and irregular words. She also tries to arouse in children what she calls "a spelling conscience" so that they will "care about using conventional spelling as a way of being courteous to readers and as a way of presenting themselves and their work in a way that will evoke the most approval and the least disapproval." But, she says with fine sophistication, "helping helps only to the point where it begins to inhibit . . . ; spelling drill and conscience help only so far. There is a point past which they make the child anxious and hesitant instead of happy and productive. There is a dynamic tension among all the helping elements, and the artistry of teaching concerns the perception of when to boost forward and when to provide time to breathe and consolidate."[7]

The cliché that one learns to write by writing applies to beginners no less than it applies to more advanced learners. If school gives them plenty of opportunity to write, they are likely to make more and better progress than if writing is only an occasional activity. The questions "how much?" and "how often?" can only be begged with the answers "much" and "often." First- or second-graders obviously cannot produce 150-word themes every day. Fifteen minutes is a long span of attention for children that age to give a single task, and by the time it is all corrected, illustrated, and copied on good paper, they may have spent several days on a story only a few sentences long. Children in fifth and sixth grades cannot generate a theme a day either. A biweekly deadline may be all that an average sixth-grader can meet and still produce decent compositions. What matters is that beginning writers be surrounded with language, and that nearly every day they do something that they recognize as related to their writing.

Underlying all the conditions that make it possible for beginners to learn, there must be the incentive to write. For children, the strongest incentive is a feeling that their writing is important, a certitude that what they write will make a difference, for better or for worse, today or tomorrow. If there remain any swains who send love letters, they know that the written outpourings of their hearts will bring favor or disfavor. Lawyers know that their briefs win or lose cases, and professional writers know that their writing will make or break them. And for children in elementary school, as Helen Danforth comments, "there must be daily and weekly payoffs in feelings of satisfaction, recognition, and sense of power." When they take home announcements or invitations that they have written and illustrated, they have greater satisfaction than when they are sent home with communications that have been mimeographed in pale purple ink by the school office. When their stories festoon classroom walls and bulletin boards, children share recognition of a very routine variety, but the child whose story is typed and bound and placed in a permanent collection in the school library enjoys a feeling of truly personal achievement. Writing to pen pals is probably enjoyable enough, but a reply from the White House to a letter asking for the president's autograph is a powerful "reinforcement" to any sixth-grader. And Dan and Jordy must have felt pretty good when their Thanksgiving piece came out in print. Everybody at the Greeley School reads *The Snooper!*

It is altogether reasonable to expect schools to provide the conditions for learning to write. That, after all, is one of the first things schools are here to do. Yet even those that provide the best conditions have only a limited amount of time for regular instruction in writing (a small fraction of the time children spend there), and conditions at home are no less important after children start school than before they enter kindergarten. When conditions in school are good, parents can help materially by taking a genuine interest in their children's learning to write. When conditions are not so good, parents can compensate, first, by making sure that their son or daughter has his or her own place to write. It doesn't have to be a professional studio. It can be an old table in somebody's room, but it does have to meet certain specifications: it must have a firm, smooth writing surface, decent light, a reliable supply of paper and pencils, and access to a pencil sharpener or someone who is willing to sharpen pencils with a knife. Then, they can encourage their youngster to use his place to practice making the letters and numbers he is learning in school, to compose stories to show or to read (perhaps a story, now, to go with that letter for grandma). Parents can always insist, when there are letters to write, that children go there to write them; and when they begin to bring assignments home, father and mother can make sure that their children do them. Parents are not always present or able to give help, but their willingness to try is important, and so is their readiness to listen to their children read what they have written. Needless to say, parents should never cease to speak with care or discontinue the custom of conversing with their children about what they do and read and watch. And if parents themselves believe that writing is important, they can usually make that fact usefully evident.

Learning to write cannot be tightly programmed, and too fine a definition of goals for children as they go from grade to grade may set a trap of expectations resulting in frustration all round. Moreover, it is well to remember that the hard thinking that produces a well-developed and organized (as against a merely correct) composition cannot be expected from most young children. It is not until the early adolescent years that formal intellection develops. On this point Carl Bereiter and his colleagues issue a useful warning: "There is a very convincing body of psychological research showing that the number of ideas people can hold in mind simultaneously is strictly limited, and that children can hold fewer in mind than adults (which is a reason for not trying to do much about logical coherence in the elementary school)."[8] While it is unwise to define objectives too precisely along the way or to presume that children's writing will approach adult logic and organization; it is reasonable to expect that when they are promoted to the seventh grade, most boys and girls will be able to write with a measure of dependable skill. If they have had sensible instruction, they should be able to spell and punctuate, to make clear and correct statements in sentences and paragraphs. They should be able to write respectable stories that have beginnings, middles, and ends; letters that have dignity if not great sophistication; accurate paraphrases of "research" in encyclopedias; news that is fit to print. In short, in their development through the secondary grades, they should have gained enough experience to become competent writers.

The Teenager as Writer

Something goes wrong in the secondary grades, however.* The situation is more depressing in the public schools than in independent schools, where writing has never lost its prominence, but even in selective preparatory schools something has been going wrong. If their development as writers does not actually regress, students in junior and senior high school seem to lose interest in writing or lose their way in learning. Those whose instruction was sensible and whose learning was sound in elementary school usually have sufficient skill to carry them over the lumpy years, but others—and, regrettably, the others have been in the majority—are passed along from grade to grade (the procedure is known as "social promotion") and sometimes graduate from high school with little more skill and less incentive to write than they had in third or fourth grade.

The schools, inevitably, are being held accountable, with a vengeance. As reports of declines in student achievement have tolled across the land, the press and the public have delighted in excoriating all schools for the failure of students to learn the basics. Here and there individual schools or school districts have even found themselves the defendants in malpractice suits. To wreak such vengeance is impertinent, but it is not altogether improper to hold the schools accountable. Perhaps due to a lack of understanding, writing has long been neglected in the schools,

---

*We use the term "secondary grades" to include grades seven through twelve.

where reading is chief among the "language arts" and writing usually subsumed into "English." Its importance thus diminished, writing has not had a fighting chance. W. Dean Memering acknowledges,

> In both the high schools and the colleges, teaching writing turns out to be anyone's guess about what to teach or how or why . . . composition is virtually not "taught" at all, and when it is taught, it is taught with little understanding of rhetorical theory; and when it is evaluated, the evaluation is not consistent with the teaching.[9]

The schools must share responsibility for this pedagogical confusion, and they must answer for their almost total reliance on multiple-choice (multiple-guess?) tests, which has practically eliminated one important use of writing. They have also to answer for the proliferation of electives and minicourses, which have made it quite possible and legitimate for students to graduate without taking any courses that require written work, much less instruction in composition. Electives follow a kind of curricular Gresham's Law, driving the hard courses out of the high school student market.

But the problem is not so simple—not even so simple as all that. It is "not that English educators have not tried," says Anne Obenchain with justification. "Millions of dollars have been spent in foundation and government-financed studies to develop sequential language programs for teacher guidance; and it is doubtful that there is a school anywhere in the country today in which members of the English department have not conscientiously planned a step-by-step development of the basic skills."[10] English teachers *have* tried, but (for reasons we shall consider in the next chapter) by and large they have not succeeded either in giving students enough incentive to write or in sustaining interest in writing long enough for them to develop competence.

It is plausible if not demonstrably probable that teenagers, being somehow more directly affected by the so-called adult culture than younger children, are peculiarly susceptible to the conditions in society that discourage people from writing. Because their coming and going is less restricted, their exposure to the world may be at once more extensive and more intensive. And, it must be said, they are—early and late—in that paradoxical part of life called adolescence. So much has been made of the lumpiness of adolescence that boys and girls in their teens are sometimes spoken of (and treated) as other than human. The physical changes that occur in adolescence are too familiar to mention and probably have nothing to do with writing. However, the emotional changes, which generously help to underwrite the practice of psychology, probably have a great deal to do with adolescents' incentive (or lack of it) to write, as well as their interest (or lack thereof).

Although not *every* youth has an identity crisis, it is safe to say that teenagers, rather more than young children and grown-ups, tend to be introspective, doubtful, and self-conscious. They commonly have enormous appetites (for new experiences, as well as for food) and, conscious now of the necessity to assert themselves, they often have a difficult time coping with the authority of adults. They are of course becoming, but not yet, adults themselves, and theirs is an especially insecure season of life.

Adolescents seem to enjoy learning the wrong things (like smoking pot) and not to enjoy learning the right things (like academic subjects), but the fact is, that most of them can, and a few of them do, learn to write respectably well. Those who do are those who have or are given incentive, as well as the discipline appropriate to the task of learning to write.

Like young children and like adults, people in their teens need to be persuaded that by writing they will achieve something that is desirable, important, or necessary. Contrary to much lay and professional opinion, they do not need to be guaranteed that anything they write about will conform to their interest of the moment. They do not have to be "grabbed" before they start. One might expect ninth-graders to turn up their noses at fairy tales as kids' stuff, but an Ulster County (New York) teacher kept 85 ninth-graders busy and apparently very happy for ten weeks learning about fairy tales and writing their own. A fourteen-year-old boy (whose story, entitled "The Mice and the Mole," was among the best) said he enjoyed the class "because it was something different. It wasn't the same old grammar we are always getting."[11] At Langley High School in Virginia, Anne Obenchain developed and taught a strictly disciplined two-year reading and writing program. Her description of the program suggests that it depended heavily on the kind of drill work that high school students are presumed to find tedious. Yet when 259 students who had just completed the course were polled anonymously, 90 percent indicated confidence in the improvement of their writing, and in voluntary comments 192 individuals "voiced strong support of the program, expressing gratitude for the skills which it had enabled them to develop," while only 25 expressed boredom or resentment.[12]

It goes without saying that in each of these cases the merits of the teacher—his or her skill, informed by knowledge and by vital interest in the subject—must have played an important part in persuading the students that by writing they would achieve something worth their time and effort. But persuaded they evidently were, and there can be no doubt that they all gained experience that increased their competence as writers.

English class is not the only place in school where students may find that writing is worth their time and effort. Teachers of other subjects have what might be called the power of incentive, and they use it to the great benefit of their students. Although the discipline of history has been drained by the spread of social studies, some teachers in history/social studies departments perceive that writing has something to do with learning, not just with communicating. Barry Beyer is one of them. Now a professor of history at Carnegie-Mellon University, Beyer began his teaching career as a high school teacher of history and social studies. He believes that all teachers have a responsibility to "teach students *how* to read, write, and think," and in an article in *Social Education*, he outlines in careful detail how social studies teachers can do this. Significantly, he first discusses writing, which, he stresses, is not an end in itself but a learning activity. He does not overlook the mechanics of writing, but believes that students experience greatest difficulty in organizing thoughts and information. He insists on the importance of giving precise directions for writing assignments and on the necessity of providing students with opportunities to "discuss, reflect on, and rewrite" what they have written.[13]

There may be teachers of every subject in secondary school who give their students incentive to write. There just aren't enough of them. Those who also give their students *discipline* in writing help—as perhaps no one else can—to further the development of those students as writers.

The first meaning of *discipline* is teaching, and it is a shame that the word has come to be so commonly associated with punishment. It is an even greater shame that so many teachers, because they do not know how to discipline students to write well, only punish them for writing poorly. They use their red pencils to mark mistakes in spelling and grammar and take off points for these mistakes, but do very little to help students write better. Some teachers, however, have the knack. Ordinarily they are not great writers themselves; but they are competent writers, and they appreciate the fact that adolescents ordinarily have much to learn in order to become as competent. It follows that they do not make a practice of springing topics on students, expecting them to produce (in twenty minutes' time) well-organized and carefully written essays, replete with examples to support ideas, and free of errors in spelling, grammar, and punctuation to boot. Rather, they have conversations with their students in which the topic is discussed for general understanding and narrowed for the practical purpose of writing. In making an assignment (whether it be a term paper, an essay, or a class exercise), they are careful to be quite specific and perfectly clear about what they expect students to do (no such muddy assignments as "The War of 1812. Discuss."). When an assignment calls for a long paper, they make provision for drafting, and they are not scandalized when the drafts have mechanical errors, not despairing when the drafts are incoherent or insubstantial. But when the chips are down and the rewritten work is handed in, they will not give full credit to any papers that are carelessly or thoughtlessly written. They may not even accept such a paper.

When adolescent writers find incentive and discipline in school, parents can easily promote the cause at home. They need not be writing experts, and if perchance they are, they had better be wary about assuming the role of superior court judge. What all parents—expert and inexpert—can contribute is interest. Their interest must, of course, be more than perfunctory. Interested parents will *read* papers their sons or daughters bring home; they will ask questions about the topic, perhaps volunteer ideas of their own. They will ask questions about the assignment to make sure they understand what the writer was expected to do. They will commend son or daughter on a job well done, but will *never* make believe that a poorly done job is well done. Interest costs very little, and parents who withhold it have to be grudging, lazy, or just plain dumb.

If there are not a great many teenagers who write on their own incentive and initiative, there are likely to be more than adults realize. In school there are editors and writers of newspapers, yearbooks, and literary magazines; there are writers of plays and filmscripts; there are even still a few debaters, who write out their arguments for or against the *Resolved*s before they speak them out. There are secretaries of school clubs and organizations who write minutes and letters, and not to be overlooked are those dependable kids who write program notes for sports events and other school spectacles. Out of school are the diarists and keepers of journals or logs, would-be poets and song-writers, and hobbyists who keep written records of the books they read or the birds they watch. There are writers of letters to the editors of real newspapers. The editorials about school spirit and the poetry young people write may be sappy; their letters to editors may disturb conservative middle-class parents; and their diaries may be too private for the eyes of adults. But parents and teachers who believe that writing matters will look for such initiative, promote it whenever they find it, and guide it insofar as they can. The light may flicker feebly, but it is the sacred flame.

It might be logical to conclude this chapter with the well-organized and carefully written essay of a twelfth-grader on some topic like "The Character of Hamlet." Such an essay is at hand, and it is evidence that some students do write with style and skill by the time they finish high school. But a thirteen-year-old girl's letter to the editor of the *New York Times* serves our purposes better. The letter comments on the *Times*'s report of a "No TV Week," which a handful of New York City parents and children endured in April 1977. Her letter fairly bursts with the kind of initiative that matters in learning to write and in becoming educated.

Living for one week without TV is nothing. I'd rather read a book anyway because you can make the hero of the story look like anything you want. TV leaves nothing to be imagined. . . . I think one of the dumbest questions from TV watchers has been, "What do you do in your spare time?" The answer is easy. I am in 4-H, I take care of a flock of chickens, I'm on the basketball team, I'm on the track team, I am taking tennis lessons, I swim, I have three pet gerbils and I go to the track field by my house and practice long jumping and high jumping. I also sometimes ride horseback with my friend. I read a lot, I do homework, I've had a poem published, I collect stamps, I've had a recorder and flute lessons, I cook a lot and I have to keep count of the food my chickens eat and the eggs they lay and write it down. See what I mean by a dumb question?[14]

Chapter 6

The Conditions of Teaching

Learning to write is conditional, and so is teaching writing. As a matter of fact, teaching anything has become a dubious undertaking in recent years. Critics who heap blame on teachers for all the shortcomings of the schools are evidently insensible of the appalling conditions that too commonly constitute the disorder of the present day in American education. Public school classrooms are crowded with boys and girls of widely differing abilities so that reduced budgets may be met and persistent notions of egalitarianism satisfied. The fractious children of a poorly disciplined society are not easily contained in classrooms, where their misbehavior is sometimes truly frightful. Teachers' hands are tied by the lengthening red tape of bureaucracy, while their tuition is constantly interrupted for the sake of activities that entertain students and please the public but educate no one.

Such conditions will not be eliminated or much changed simply by the restoration of strictness to the classroom. And while teachers of all subjects are obliged to work under them, these circumstances may be peculiarly arduous for those who are expected to teach writing—for the most part, teachers of English.

What English Teachers Face

The greatest difficulty English teachers face—at least, the difficulty that evokes the loudest and most plausible complaints—is overload: classes with more students than a teacher can teach. To teach writing one must set students to writing, of course. That means papers to correct, and correcting writing is rarely a simple matter of toting up mistakes and scoring. Correcting ordinarily entails careful reading, making critical comments, and evaluating—a time-consuming procedure and, because in writing right and wrong are seldom white and black, an exacting one. Correcting becomes a staggering and sometimes hopeless task when classes are crowded, and crowded classes tend to be the rule rather than the exception. "The number of students most secondary teachers work with, or against," Joan Grady told us with a dash of bitters, "is about 150. That is the case where the load per class is 30 and the teaching day includes only five classes." Two short papers a week would seem to be a modest but reasonable expectation of junior and senior high school students who are learning to write. Turn the expectation around, however, and it ceases to be anything like modest or reasonable. If it takes an average of seven minutes to correct a 150-word composition (and it does), a teacher with 30 students in each of five classes would have to devote 158 entire schooldays a year to correcting papers—with no coffee breaks or lunch hours.

Teachers are expected not only to cope with excessive numbers, but also to accommodate pupils of such widely differing abilities that they honestly do not know how to begin or where to set hand. Here is the way a middle school teacher describes her seventh-grade class of thirty-six:

> One has an I.Q. of about 78, one of about 90, and one is really subfunctional! About eight have skills in reading and writing of third-graders. They are unmotivated and rarely hand in work. About 15 are just average: they try; they write poorly, but *can* write; they can and do read. Then there are eight who are above average and two who are exceptional. I find it difficult to provide them with suitable work, and they have not responded to independent assignments.[1]

Commenting on the difficulty of coping with all her five classes, the same teacher says, "Individualized instruction is an ideal, but for 175 kids? Teaching these classes is a compromise in every way."

The imposition of nonteaching chores on all schoolteachers is mirrored nicely by a sardonic "observer" who wrote the following letter to the editor of the *Claremont* (California) *Courier:*

> To the Editor:
> I submit this letter because education is under fire these days. I have a suggestion that might help. I propose that one

week be set aside during which teachers would teach their routine classes and nothing extra be added.

During that week there would be no class meeting, no California Achievement Tests, no yearbook and ring sales, no senior pictures taken, no rock band assemblies, no field trips, no school fair, no play rehearsal, no track meet, no creative arts festival, no eye testing, no reading system salesman, no gym floor varnishing, no meeting for the group going to Spain, no fire drill, no pep rally, no speaker from Africa, no slide-show assembly, no TB skin test, no open-house visiting, no band practice, no passes for students to stay and finish an experiment, wait for the sweet rolls to come out of the oven, make up a test, mop up spilled paint or clean the ink off the printing press, and no early dismissal for part-time jobs.

This week should not contain Memorial Day, Good Friday, Columbus Day, Veterans' Day, Martin Luther King Day, George Washington's birthday, Labor Day, the first day it snows or the first balmy day in spring. Should such a week be arranged, it is possible that our students might be able to do what they are supposed to do in school. Learn something.

Observer[2]

Because they are presumed to be experts on writing, English teachers are the natural prey of administrators who need faculty advisers to school newspapers and other publications. Indeed, their presumed expertise with the language as it is written, read, and spoken is likely to put them first in the way of all sorts of duties and odd jobs—coaching dramatics and debating, teaching speech and public speaking, writing "behavioral objectives," taking minutes at faculty and committee meetings, and so on and on. Where language is the medium, there you are almost certain to find an English teacher nailed for an extra duty. It may be too much to say that English teachers are the beasts of school burden, but they have high vulnerability to appointment when "volunteers" are needed.

When education is reported to be in decline on every front, the shadow of suspicion falls on all schoolteachers, but English teachers may feel public distrust more poignantly than others.

Reading and writing come before arithmetic in the familiar trivium, and the shortcomings of students who cannot spell or write decent sentences seem somehow more glaring, if not actually more serious, than their limitations in mathematics or science. English teachers are not yet branded with an I for Irresponsibility as Hester Prynne was with an A for Adultery; but the pressure is on, and they feel it as it comes down from school boards through principals' offices to their classrooms. The pressure may prove good for English teachers, but surely it makes the conditions of their teaching even more difficult than it has been since education became a form of mass production.

As someone has remarked, English teaching is not a profession but a predicament.

Teachers as Writers

Where can teachers turn in their predicament? Where can they set hand? How do they begin? They can and should begin by writing. They will not reduce class size by writing, or remove any of the external conditions that keep teachers at a disadvantage. But they may gain the indispensable advantage of confidence in their own ability to write.

If all English teachers were the writing experts they are presumed to be, the national struggle for literacy would be appreciably less formidable. Some are experts, and we have them to thank for the fact that matters are no worse. But many—a great many—are not good writers, and they are often candid enough to say so. They have had precious little practice in writing and, as a rule, no training to teach writing.

Few adults who were educated during the 1950s and 1960s did much writing when they were in school. Those were the years when the quantity of students to be educated overtook the quality of the education they received, and multiple-choice exams took the place of essay writing. In college they *may* have had some writing instruction in a required freshman English class, but if they went on to major in English, that was probably literature. They may have become knowledgeable and avid readers, but their development as writers went by the board. The younger the adult today, the less likely he is to have had much useful or reliable writing experience in school and college. Discipline in learning to write was ushered out when the era of innovations, with all its options and electives, was ushered in.

One might expect something different of teacher training institutions. As far as writing goes, however, teacher education has been out to lunch for years. A senior majoring in elementary education in one of the country's more reputable teacher training institutions was frank enough to say that her courses had required virtually no writing on her part and that she had had no specific preparation whatsoever for teaching writing. It may be that professors of education have been so occupied for so long with methods of teaching reading that the necessity and virtue of teaching writing have escaped their notice. Whatever the explanation, over the years the departments, schools, and colleges of education have done pathetically little to prepare schoolteachers to appreciate that virtue or to meet the necessity.

It happens, then, through no fault of their own, that teachers come to school poorly equipped to teach writing. Nor are they likely to be much interested in doing so. What they remember of their own experience (if anything) is learning grammar and the rest of it by drill, and they have neither wish nor conscience to inflict the dull, difficult business on their students. Small wonder that as the prisoner leaps to loose his chains, the English teacher jumps for joy when research shows that instruction in grammar does not contribute to the improvement of student writing. They would prefer to teach literature.

But they are expected to teach literature *and* writing. The predicament again.

Enjoyment is the mainspring of good teaching. When teachers discover for themselves that they can derive a great deal of enjoyment and satisfaction in writing, they can teach writing with enjoyment and satisfaction. And no teacher has to look far to make the discovery. Something as homely as a lesson plan can serve the purpose. Just to compose one's thoughts in writing is a satisfaction, and writing is an excellent way—perhaps the very best way—to do precisely that. A lesson plan written out in complete sentences and in thoughtful detail can bring to teaching the satisfaction of a composed mind, the enjoyment of sound preparation. The chore of writing reports can become interesting if one strives to communicate clearly and concisely with a principal, let us say, or a parent. (The easy but ineffectual way to write a report is to lard it with pretentious language and the jargon of education.)

People who keep journals or write personal letters know that writing is a valuable means of self-discovery. Such writing has a way of constraining one to be honest. Whereas in conversation one tends to "play it by ear," most people hesitate to put in writing statements that are not true. As one sorts his experience in a journal or in letters, he becomes sure of what he knows (and doesn't know), conscious of what he truly believes, confident of what he wants to do. The description of a middle school teacher's seventh-grade class on page 106 was taken from correspondence with a young woman who turned to letter-writing deliberately to improve her "composition and communications skills." Her letters reflect the improvement of those skills. They also reveal much that she learned about herself as a person and as a teacher in the course of writing them. And if writing them took time she could ill afford to spend, she was repaid by the confidence she gained as she had to cope, day by day, with 175 children whose abilities ranged from subfunctional to exceptional.

There is another good and important reason why teachers should write. Ken Donelson puts it bluntly in the *English Journal:* "Any English teacher who teaches writing but who does not write is an intellectual and pedagogical fraud."[3] In our book, that goes for the teacher of any subject who assigns written work to students. Lucy McCormick Calkins, a Connecticut elementary school teacher, says this:

> Writing is the hardest thing I do. I let my children know this. I tell them that, after a long weekend of writing, my whole jaw aches from being clenched. And at school, I write alongside my children. They see my struggles. They notice the pile of crumpled starts on the floor beside me. They watch as I wrestle to find a way to tackle my subjects. They watch, and they begin to understand. Writing is not magic; it's hard work.[4]

Teachers should do the same sorts of writing their students do—the same assignments, in fact. If they do, they will be better able to gauge the difficulty of assignments, and their expectations of what students can accomplish will be more accurate (and perhaps more generous) than those of teachers who do not write. They will be able to discuss the specific issues and problems raised by assignments and discuss them with involvement. And their involvement will pay a dividend: students feel closer to teachers who write because assignments are not merely handed down to them. Teachers need not write every assignment, to be sure, but the more they can take on, the greater the rewards for themselves and for their students.

It is not enough to urge teachers to do more writing. Certain research shows that the mere act of writing does not necessarily result in a testable improvement in writing skill. Moreover, experts, presumed or real, are usually wise to turn to others for suggestion and instruction. Medical doctors have their physicians, opera and tennis stars their coaches, and teachers of writing can afford literary advisers. It doesn't take a search committee to find one. Advisers need not be teachers themselves or professional writers. They need only know the difference between good and not-so-good writing; be willing to be candid; and make comments and suggestions as their advisees write lesson plans, reports, and the same papers their students will write.

That is a good suggestion, although it is easier to make than to follow. Perhaps the most comfortable and most constructive thing a teacher can do is take part in one of the writing programs growing up in today's climate of concern. Prominent among these are the Bay Area Writing Project (described on pages 132–136) and its many spin-offs. Others are now in operation, and the prospect is that before much longer good programs will be widely enough available to make it practicable for teachers, working together under the guidance of seasoned peers, to develop expertise as writers and teachers of writing. Teachers should be able to get information about these programs by following the journals and watching bulletin boards.

College professors publish or perish, but there is no pressing reason why schoolteachers have to write for publication—unless the pressure comes from within. Countless schoolteachers do write and publish, and among them are successful writers of fiction and poetry. Textbook authors are usually teachers who cannot repress enthusiasm for their own way of teaching a subject, and the professional journals depend on teachers who have insights to share. More power to them all. They are probably better teachers for the writing they publish.

Teaching Writing and Literature

Teaching literature and writing need not be an either/or proposition. Perhaps the obvious way to teach literature is to set students to reading, discuss the reading with them, and test them on it. The testing can be done with multiple-choice questions. When students are also set to *writing*, however, they learn more about what they read. "The Character of Hamlet" (which we did not expose at the conclusion of Chapter 5) as an essay topic not only tests students' knowledge of the play, but also gives them an opportunity to deepen their understanding. When a teacher leads students into a problem to solve or an idea to develop in writing (for example, "Show that Macbeth's ambition was vaulting"), the learning may be even sounder.

English teachers often use models from literature in teaching writing. When this practice becomes a joyless exercise, teachers must be doing something wrong. They may suppose that literary models are to be taken only from what the chairman of our commission calls "fuddy-duddy classics" (poor old *Silas Marner*), or perhaps they confuse emulation and imitation.

Literary models must not be too remote from the student's own world view. An essay by Francis Bacon is in certain respects a model of composition, but students may exhaust their energy merely in overcoming the obstacle of its being a period piece. An essay by E. B. White, equally a model of composition, does not interpose this obstacle. Not that models must be confined to the contemporary. Common sense should come into play: Montaigne is probably useless to the composition teacher, but works written several generations later (such as Hazlitt's "On My First Acquaintance with Poets") may be perfectly usable. Subject to the qualifications expressed above, the model must be excellent of its kind. It should be chosen not merely because it is "relevant" to students' transient interests, but because it is in itself a good piece of writing. The model should interest them not because it deals with rock music, but because it deals with rock music lucidly and concisely.

The Hazlitt essay cited above is quite long. But teachers can find good teaching opportunities in shorter models. One of our commissioners told us that, as a young high school teacher, he decided to spend a whole period on the study of *a single sentence.* He chose the sentence ending Conrad's story "Youth." Here it is:

And we all nodded at him: the man of finance, the man of accounts, the man of law, we all nodded at him over the polished table that like a still sheet of brown water reflected our faces, lined, wrinkled; our faces marked by toil, by deceptions, by success, by love; our weary eyes looking still, looking always, looking anxiously for something out of life, that while it is expected is already gone—has passed unseen, in a sigh, in a flash—together with the youth, with the strength, with the romance of illusions.[5]

First he retold the story for the benefit of those who had not read it. Then, during the remainder of the fifty-minute period, every one of the complex elements fused in this beautiful sentence was discovered and discussed by the class: rhythm, organization, imagery, summatory power, economy, sound, diction, punctuation—and emotional effect. At no time did the teacher mention that it was good "literature." The discussion was severely restricted to the analysis of the sentence as a sentence. But by the end of the hour the students had unconsciously come to the conclusion that this *was* good writing—call it literature, if you like.

Probably those students would never in their lives produce a sentence as good. But they were fired with enthusiasm. Enthusiasm for what? Of all dull things, the construction, even the mechanics, of an English sentence! What they found out was that a single sentence, if well composed, has a high energy content, does a deal of work. None of them was asked to imitate Conrad, but most of them were touched, if only temporarily, by the pure passion of emulation.

Writing and Other Subjects

Teachers of other subjects ought to assign writing—and write—not to help English teachers do their jobs, but to do their own jobs better.

One who began his career as a teacher of history likes to recount two successive revelations he had a good many years ago, just when he was coming to think of himself as a pretty good teacher, if not a rising faculty star. Looking soberly at a set of papers one day, he was given to see that if what his students had written represented what they knew and understood about history, perhaps he wasn't such a promising teacher after all. Self-inflicted though the wound was, wounded pride drove him to spend much of his time showing students how to write papers for history. Before long he had the second revelation. He realized that his students were not just learning to write; they were writing to learn. When the demands of clear composition left them no alternative to being precise (not approximate), substantial (not vague), and orderly (not hit-or-miss), his students began not only to remember "the facts," but also to understand them, to be able to use them. In short, they began to know what they were talking about.

Granted, it is not easy to imagine ways one might use writing in physical education or home economics classes. It's not easy, but it's not impossible, either. Certainly teachers of history and social studies should have no difficulty improvising ways. Barry Beyer, in his article "Teaching the Basics in Social Studies" (see page 101), makes suggestions social studies teachers can follow.[6]

Some science teachers do recognize that "no matter how well a student understands a scientific concept or regardless of how well he or she may have done an experiment, unless that student can explain the concept or experiment clearly, something will be lost, and it may be that he or she does not, in fact, understand either the concept or the experiment very well."[7] So says E. Fred Carlisle as guest editor of the *English Journal* in an issue devoted to the interest in writing shared by English and science teachers. Teachers of the arts might find their students more knowledgeable and even more creative if they set them to writing from time to time. Teachers of physical education could help to meet public demand for cardiopulmonary resuscitation training in the schools by assigning essays on that subject, while teachers of home economics might set their students to writing cookbooks. Why not?

Team Teaching

Team teaching can be exploited both to advance learning on a broader front and to serve the end of good writing. Effective team teaching calls for sophistication as well as cooperation, however. We do not recommend, for instance, that English and History agree on a topic, then further agree that History grade the papers on "content" and English grade them on mechanics, organization, and style. As we have said before, the content of good writing is not just an aggregate of facts and figures and really cannot be separated from mechanics, organization, and style. To divide the labor of team teachers in this way is to make a fatal distinction. History would not be disabused of the mistaken notion that writing is "not my department"; English would be left to complain that teaching writing is dull and dreary work; and students would be carried along in the ever-rolling stream of wrong-headed writing discipline.

If, however, the history (or science, math, French, music, art, or another) teacher writes; if the English teacher knows, or is willing to learn, something about history or the other subjects; and if both are blessed with imagination, then those teachers can come up with assignments and projects that truly *will* advance learning on a broad front, give students unusually good experience in writing, and in the bargain make teaching more interesting and less burdensome. Whatever writing the students do should be an integral part of the project, and the teachers should have integrity as a team. That is, they should share, not divide, the responsibility, even in grading.

First Aid

Teachers who determine to do something about their own writing (and do it) are certain to benefit—but not soon enough to cope with tomorrow morning's classes. There is no magic to make hard-pressed teachers instantly happy and forever effective, but suggestions follow that might make a difference in teaching 150 assorted students.

Teachers who find correcting papers the hardest cross to bear cannot very well drop the cross and forget it, but they can learn to carry it more efficiently. Some conscientious people feel guilty when they do not read every paper that every student writes, correct every mistake, give the paper a grade, and return it promptly—with comments. Conscientiousness is a hallmark of good schoolteaching, but such a degree of conscientiousness tends to be self-defeating. It is simply not possible to do all that when one has to cope with 150 students and their papers.

However, there are several constructive alternatives open to teachers to relieve the difficulty of correcting.

Proposing that teachers devote more time to students' preparation for writing and to rewriting is not to offer a gimmick with which to parlay one assignment into two or three. Giving more time to preparation and rewriting may seem like a gimmick because this strategy makes the quantity of papers less staggering, but these two—preparation and writing—are the most important functions of what we call, simply, writing. Just as the elementary teacher engages third-graders in conversation about goblins, so a secondary teacher can prime students for writing by discussing with them (not talking to them) the topic on which they are to write. After a class period (more or less—there is seldom the hurry that teachers imagine) of discussion, students can be assigned to produce papers in draft form (draft, not outline). Accepting the drafts as one assignment, the teacher can *mark* them (that is, note mistakes and make suggestions for improvement) and assign rewriting next. Then, with a minimum of marking, the teacher can *grade* the rewritten papers. Discussion, drafting, and rewriting take important time, but it is needed time that, all too often, is abbreviated if not altogether eliminated.

In an interesting paper, "Composition and the Editorial Process," Wallace W. Douglas sensibly reminds us of something teachers frequently forget: that the act of writing is an elusive operational process, not a mechanical response to a neatly stated problem. Much of it, he says, may go on below the threshold of consciousness. Therefore the young writer cannot always "observe the carefully ordered rules of the classroom." Douglas suggests turning "the composition classroom into an editor's office and the composition class into an editorial conference."[8] He stresses drafting and rewriting. Writing a *draft* is one thing, he points out, and a good thing; but asking students to produce a *finished paper* is quite another. Discussion of a first draft should emphasize material; discussion of a second draft, organization and form. Douglas would leave questions of mechanics to a third draft. His paper is well worth reading as a discussion of the *operational* character of writing, as against the mere demanding and correcting of one-phase compositions.

The mistakes customarily marked by teachers are mechanical errors in spelling, punctuation, and grammar; teachers often pay relentless attention to them. It is easy to do this because such mistakes are patently mistakes—wrong, not right—and marking them may give teachers a feeling of power or security. They *know* the mistakes are wrong, and by marking them they *do* something. Though this kind of marking may indeed give teachers a feeling of security, the hard-hitting approach has a way of making students feel insecure and may very well distract them from the intellectual effort that is the condition of competent writing. At times, ignoring mechanics can prove useful. At other times it is useful to mark only one or two kinds of mistakes; that method should draw on the time and intelligence of students, not teachers.

Courtney Cazden comments pointedly on the overvaluing of mechanics: "The most serious problem . . . is . . . an imbalance between too much attention to drill on the component skills of language and literacy and too little attention to their significant use."[9] Still, we must not conclude that we can place mechanics permanently on the back burner. We should ask ourselves at what point or points in the curriculum mechanics should be stressed, how much attention they merit when one is discussing a specific composition, and especially what methods exist for teaching them effectively. Bereiter and his colleagues remind us of one such method—taking dictation: "A method now much out of fashion, but one that could evidently be lively and profitable when handled with care. . . . It has the advantage and disadvantage that it allows full concentration on mechanics, without having to worry about generating content."[10]

Because students need to know where they go wrong and where they fall short, teachers should, as a rule, mark papers and return them promptly. But to benefit from writing, students do not need always to have papers marked and returned. They do need to know that from time to time their papers will not be marked or returned. In this connection there is value in having students keep journals in which they write every day (a paragraph or a few sentences) with never a teacher's mark or a grade—only occasional perusal and acknowledgment.

Few comments are worth the time it takes to write them, but teachers tend to be compulsive and write many. Meticulous students may chew and even digest them, but the ordinary schoolboy or girl will scarcely taste them. Says Paul Kalkstein,

"Many teachers moan that students are interested only in the grade, not in their comments, but who is to blame the student who wants to know what his paper is worth."[11] Occasionally the thoughtful written comment of a teacher serves a constructive purpose—especially if the comment is one of favorable criticism. More often, writing comments wastes a teacher's valuable time. More can be accomplished, and more quickly accomplished, in a moment's discussion with a student.

One way to lighten the burden of correcting, to be sure, is to assign fewer compositions. We are dead set against that, however, because to require students (even 150 of them) to write less often than once a week would be to proceed in the wrong direction. If computers could think, the day might come when computer-assisted correcting would solve the problem. But since they can't and it won't, the only way a teacher can effectually reduce the volume of paper-correcting work is to enlist help. Good students are sometimes enlisted, and many classrooms now have paraprofessional or volunteer aides. Although students can help (and learn) by marking mechanical errors, we have reservations about deputizing students to *grade* their classmates' compositions, and we are wary of using aides for this purpose. Not opposed but wary, since to mark and grade student writing, an aide must be carefully and thoroughly trained by the classroom teacher.

Students can be very perceptive and constructively critical, and they learn more about writing from each other than doubtful teachers might imagine. They can't learn everything, to be sure; but working together on their own sometimes gives them incentive, and such self-instruction may be one effective way to lighten the burden of correcting. In the 1976 edition of his popular *Hooked on Books*, Daniel Fader describes a scheme of grouping students to teach themselves writing. The scheme is rather complicated; but Fader (who has tried to come realistically to grips with the difficulty of overload) swears it works, and it is surely worth considering.[12]

Grading student writing is often an exacting and baffling responsibility. Errors in grammar, spelling, and punctuation are easily identified and scored, as we have noted. When it comes to the development of ideas, however, and to matters of coherence and organization and questions of style, right and wrong are seldom, if ever, absolute. Lacking clear and concrete criteria, the teacher who wants to approximate a "holistic" evaluation of student writing can be quickly put to confusion. Although good writing, like a living creature, cannot ultimately be taken apart and retain its vitality, different aspects of a composition can be appraised. Suppose, for example, these aspects are defined as content (development of ideas, use of details and facts), organization by sequential paragraphs, style (vocabulary, idiom, sentence variety, and imaginative "touches"), and mechanics. A teacher might put a value of 50 on content, 25 on organization and style, and 25 on mechanics. If content is the principal concern, it might be valued at 75, with a total of 25 for all the rest, or 100 on content and forget the rest this time. A teacher who wants to stress spelling, punctuation, and grammar can put more or all of the premium on mechanics. Again, students need to know what their teacher is up to. Mutual understanding is always the nexus of good teaching and sound learning.

There is, we say again, no magic. Nor do the suggestions here make any pretense at being infallible or comprehensive. If they help to improve conditions for any teacher, they have served their purpose.

Chapter 7

The Outlook

Out of the night that covers us there is emerging not broad daylight, but enough light for most people to see that something is wrong with the writing of our citizenry and that, whatever the something is, it isn't good for us. In our republic, initiative at the summit often betokens national awareness of a problem. We took as a good sign Jimmy Carter's pledge to communicate with the American people "in plain English for a change." The president himself set the standard by speaking, as James Reston observed, "in sentences, thinking between commas, without a subject or a predicate out of place."[1] Carter's administration was apparently influenced by the presidential example. Soon after his appointment, Secretary Harris started a "write it right" campaign in the Department of Housing and Urban Development. Secretary Califano committed Health, Education and Welfare to a five-year project (a conservative time estimate, at best) to rewrite that department's rules. Eight hundred federal employees turned out for a 1977 seminar (organized, appropriately, by the National Center for Administrative Justice) devoted to rewriting government regulations, of which some twenty thousand pages are produced each year, to the confusion of Americans who are to be regulated. Even the Internal Revenue Service promised to make income tax forms intelligible.

When Alfred Kahn went to Washington as chairman of the Civil Aeronautics Bureau, he made this reasonable but probably unprecedented request of his staff:

> May I ask you, please, to try very hard to write Board orders and, even more so, drafts of letters for my signature, in straightforward, quasi-conversational, humane prose—as though you are talking to or communicating with real people?[2]

If people in the federal government are worried that the country won't be run well unless those at the top write well, those in the middle and at the bottom had better sit up and take notice. And that is what they are doing. It is a fact that poor old Johnny still can't write, but his parents and teachers are getting the word and are becoming determined to make sure that he learns.

Back to the Basics

In a democratic country, hope for constructive action is most solidly based when the citizenry seems to be expressing a general will. The back-to-basics movement does appear to be the expression of something akin to the general will. Even though it is not universally favored or even fully understood by all, it is the clearest signal yet received that something must be done.

Unlike the struggle of the 1960s for civil rights and the advance of women for their rights in the 1970s, the trend toward basics in education is not an organized effort with single-minded leaders and dedicated followers. It is simply the result of thousands or millions of people becoming convinced that education is seriously deficient both in discipline and in substance.

It should be said at once that the phrase-maker whose gift for alliteration provided the movement with its title performed no service. To imply or to permit the inference that the current ground swell of dissatisfaction is nothing more than wrong-headed nostalgia for one-room schoolhouses staffed with strict, old-fashioned marms is to do many thoughtful people a great disservice. It is also to ignore the widespread, deep concern for the adequacy of *college* education, which must be recognized as part of the ground swell of the new trend in our thinking.

Those in the movement or for the movement are, for the most part, people who are fed up with beguiling innovations, with the failure of kids in school to learn much about English, history, math, and science, and with the failure of college undergraduates to gain much besides fragments of knowledge and understanding. Those in the movement are persuaded now (if they were not before) that sound learning entails hard work. They are also absolutely appalled at the poor quality of writing common among today's school and college graduates. Among the proponents are some who talk and behave as if discipline were more a matter of breaking spirits than of training minds; some whose purpose, patently, is indoctrination, not transmission of the culture; and some who simplistically reduce education to the proverbial and perennial three Rs. Some, but comparatively few. By and large, these are sensible people, who want value for their tax dollars and tuition fees, or return for their investment of scholarship and teaching.

Ranged against them are those who sincerely distrust the "back-to-basics mentality." Opponents fear that emphasis on the basics will result in underemphasis on other subjects or their elimination as frills. Some are afraid that the schools, zealous to drill grammar, spelling, and punctuation into the heads of children, will lose sight of the fact that there are different learning styles. Opponents are apprehensive of what they see as the danger of discipline so strict that education will be dehumanized. Among them are the militant antigrammarians, anxious to hold their beachhead, and evidently some who just enjoy sneering— the *English Journal's* "roving editor," for instance, who affects a lower-case style to speak his mind.

> when you look at the flocking around the "basics," you see a striking similarity among those birds. you may have heard about the curious breed of bird (now, alas, not yet extinct) that demonstrated the ability to fly backwards in a diminishing spiral causing it to disappear into its own fundament. the basic fundamentalists are a similar breed, on a similar course. the problems seem to be that they are related to the vulture family and survive by feeding on dead things—including dead ideas.[3]

In spite of doubters and detractors, the movement has gained strength as concern about student achievement has spread. Under pressure from without, many colleges and schools are at least doing something about it, and probably just as many have been moved from within. In the colleges, measures range from tests separating entering freshmen who can write from those who can't to proposals for overhauling curricula. By overwhelming vote, Harvard's Faculty of Arts and Sciences voted in 1978 to adopt

Dean Henry Rosovsky's proposal intended to assure that when students graduate they will be literate in major forms of intellectual discourse. And, commenting on the action, Edward Fiske said in the *New York Times*, "Harvard is the latest, and in many ways the most visible and significant, in a series of major liberal arts faculties across the country to introduce more structure and coherence to undergraduate curriculums."[4] Dean Rosovsky's proposal calls, by the way, for students to demonstrate competence in writing, in math, and in a foreign language. (Such a demand doubtless implies an adherence to the roving editor's "dead ideas.")

Understandably, much more about the basics is seen and heard in elementary and secondary education. It would be difficult to find a school unaffected by the movement, although some school people protest (perhaps too loudly) that they cannot go back to the basics because they have never left them. Greater emphasis (if not always the best kind) is being placed on reading, writing, and arithmetic in elementary schools, and secondary schools are having second thoughts about permitting students to earn diplomas by means of watered-down or frivolous courses. Here and there "alternative schools" (variously called "traditional," "fundamental," or simply "basic") have been opened to redress the balance by decreasing the time and attention paid to many of the electives and "minicourses" that have crowded school programs in recent years, often at the expense of basic education.

In the opinion of many, distrust of electives lies at the heart of the movement. The proliferation of electives is based on the notion that the student's theory of education (teach me what for the moment interests me) is to be accepted. The back-to-basics notion is that every child must be taught the rudiments that make for an educated person. These rudiments may be variously taught and stressed, but in general they include solid instruction in literature, composition, mathematics, history, geography, the sciences, at least one foreign language, and some art and music. If these subjects are to be taught well, little time or money will be available for courses in the significance of the detective story and bachelor economics.

The movement's most publicized and probably its most controversial manifestation has been the introduction of minimum competency requirements in the schools. As a result of legislative action or action by state school boards, more than half the states have adopted some form of minimum-competency program. Typically, a program includes the definition of achievement standards that students must meet in reading, writing, and mathematics in order to be promoted through the grades or graduated from high school; tests to determine whether or not students do in fact qualify for promotion or graduation; and "remediation" for those who fail to qualify.

A few states have voted minimum competency requirements down, and the National Council of Teachers of English has gone on record against legislatively mandated competency testing until it "is determined to be socially and educationally beneficial."[5] There are arguments to be made against competency testing, especially when it is politically conceived. Nor do we have any illusion that by taking these tests girls and boys are going to become competent writers. However, the tests, together with even the minimal standards they are designed to serve, should lay a floor under the quality of writing in the schools. Perhaps only a subfloor, but more of a platform than many schools now have on which to start building. Although some students will find the tests preposterously easy, those who do not may be prompted to learn enough to pass them. And if the task of providing "remediation" proves boring or burdensome for teachers, perhaps it will drive them to teach in ways that will reduce the need for it in the future.

The back-to-basics movement does not provide all the answers, because it is not a program of specific reforms. But it has created a climate conducive to reform. One college teacher has commented, "If 'back to the basics' means anything at all, it should mean a return to the expectation that every teacher in every subject area is first of all a teacher of writing and reading."[6]

In the Classroom

"Remediation" is what educators are now pleased to call instruction intended to overcome deficiencies in reading, writing, and mathematics skills. The term represents what has become a familiar enterprise in American education: the effort to provide remedies for the failure of students to learn and the failure of schools to teach basic skills. Many if not most schools have always striven, with special classes, extra help, and tutoring, to accommodate the needs of students who are in arrears. After the Elementary and Secondary Education Act of 1965 recognized and attempted to provide for "disadvantaged" students, remediation became a massive enterprise costing more than $2 billion a year. Soon, even the word *massive* may be inadequate to describe the enterprise, because as state after state adopts minimum-competency requirements, requirements for the remediation of all who fail are also prescribed.

Although it is not reform, clearly remediation must be done, and the trials and errors of remediators may very well provide clues for reformers. However, it would not be realistic to expect remediation alone to bring about much if any improvement in the general state of writing. For one thing, remediation is ordinarily conceived for "communications skills" in general, not for writing in particular. When minimum competency is involved, remediation is calculated only to enable students to meet standards that tend to be embarrassingly low—no more than necessary, in other words, for students to pass the competency test, even if they have to take it two or three times. The performance of Florida's eleventh-graders taking that state's first literacy test was so deplorable (especially in mathematics) that a university mathematician was recruited to help produce a manual "replete with sample questions, suggestions for teachers to help students, and *for students to take the test.*"[7]

In the wake of Florida's first experience with "mandated" minimum-competency testing, a state legislator who is also a schoolteacher discreetly observed that "remediation has its limits."[8] Massive or miniscule, remediation costs much and accomplishes little. To regret the necessity is not to gainsay it, but there can be little doubt that over the long haul the investment of teachers' time and taxpayers' money in sound *new* programs of writing instruction will accomplish more and cost less.

While schools across the country are struggling to cope with the task of remediation, here and there local school districts or individual schools are facing up to the need to reform their teaching of writing. In a few instances there may be need for little more than "tightening up," but probably more often than not schools are finding that they have to go back to the very beginning. Information about new programs is still too limited to allow for a comprehensive survey, and few of these programs are ready yet for the kind of evaluation that yields the "hard data" generally required for the "decision-making process" these days. Nevertheless, it is possible here to identify several that appear to have distinctive merits.

The approach taken by Lucille Murray and her teachers at the Samuel Greeley School in Winnetka (see page 90) is almost too sensible to be solemnized as a program, but there it is, and we have suggested that it may be an optimum arrangement. Certainly it is an approach that might be taken by other schools, especially when the number of teachers and students is comparatively small. The principal of the Charles Ashley School in New Bedford (see p. 91) is setting a very respectable example for elementary schools that enroll students from urban, blue-collar communities and that do not have Robert Gundlachs around the corner.

Not far from New Bedford—in Dartmouth, Massachusetts—a district with four elementary schools, a middle school, and a high school has picked up its English curriculum and started to walk toward a program that ought to improve student writing. If improvement is still some distance down the road, the Dartmouth endeavor is nevertheless an example of the careful overhaul of curriculum that many schools must take before competent writing can be reasonably expected of students.

A teacher of English and department chairman before he became assistant principal of the Dartmouth High School, Arthur Bennett has been responsible for revision of the district's K–8 English curriculum. The first step was to determine objectives. A group of eighteen teachers, meeting during the summers and from time to time during the school year, labored to produce objectives. The result of their work is a fifty-six page document, divided into sections (K–3, 4–6, 7–8), with clear statements of objectives in punctuation, capitalization, grammar, and usage. Significant are the reminders in each section that "the objectives listed in this booklet represent *minimum* levels of achievement" and the injunction that teachers "are expected to assess the abilities, needs and interests of their students and supplement the minimums accordingly."[9] Adopted for use in the school year 1974–1975, the performance objectives were revised in 1976. Criterion-referenced tests are used to assess the results, and Bennett has no fear that Dartmouth teachers will allow minimum levels of achievement to become maximum.

At this writing, the next step is underway—to develop goals for the teaching of writing. Developing performance objectives, Mr. Bennett grants, is a more difficult job. "Writing can be taught," says their position paper. "While we cannot turn a student without natural writing talents into a prize-winning author, we *can* improve his writing skills." Ultimately, the plans developed for Dartmouth's elementary grades will suggest the form and content of writing instruction in the high school. Meantime, all eleventh-grade college preparatory students are being required to take a one-semester course in writing under the tuition of a teacher whose master's degree (MFA) is in writing. The classes will average twenty students, and meet three full periods a week.

In Fairfax County, Virginia, bordering on the District of Columbia, the schools have identified the improvement of writing as a major objective and given all teachers responsibility for bringing about the improvement. The *Fairfax Schools Bulletin* tells how teachers of all subjects will participate:

> When schools identify student improvement in writing as a major objective in their Commitment to Education, all teachers become instrumental in a school's writing program. The amount of writing and the kinds of writing done in all subject areas are assessed to determine to what extent English language arts classes can help prepare students for those assignments. Style guidelines for writing can be established schoolwide, and all teachers feel a sense of responsibility for improving student writing.[10]

To help teachers at this task, the county's Department of Instructional Services has prepared a *Guide for Teaching Writing*. Although cast in the military manner of behavioral objectives ("The student will use abbreviations correctly") and written in the lethal prose of educationists ("Within each grade level, the skills are correlated to reflect their integration with the writing process"), the guide is impressive as an attempt to put reliable tools for teaching writing in the hands of all the teachers of a large school district. It puts considerable emphasis on correctness, but it also presents writing as a process rather than a mechanical function. Those with the time, patience, and imagination to follow this remarkable teaching guide will undoubtedly contribute to the improvement of the writing of public school students in Fairfax County.

Building a Writing Program

To suggest that all schools follow these examples and work out their own salvations may be to fly in the face of comfortable custom. It is the increasingly well established custom of school administrators to buy, and of schoolteachers to use, commercially "packaged" programs of instruction, which come fully equipped with "behavioral objectives," "pretests," "instructional materials," and "posttests." Some such packaged programs are quite good, others are not. Some schools use them sensibly and constructively; others use them because they have no good alternative. It is safe to predict that the producers of packages will exploit the writing crisis by filling the market with programs to meet a growing demand, but we earnestly encourage schools to develop their own programs.

Hear what uncomfortable words the directors of the Bay Area Writing Project have to say: "The reinvention of the wheel is an important principle of learning in in-service programs. . . . Successful implementation of an approach requires that local teachers write their own materials."[11] To that we say, "Amen," and hasten to add that a proper writing program—one that really works—cannot represent only the efforts of a few lonely English teachers. It must be a schoolwide effort. If students are to become competent writers, composition must be recognized and treated as a discipline in its own right, lifted out of the vague, catch-all "English" course and made an interdepartmental discipline. English departments may take primary, but not exclusive, responsibility.

The first step in building a program is to bring about agreement on the general aims and standards a school believes it should meet in teaching writing. It is significant that in both Ashley School and Greeley School the first step was taken by the principal. This is not to imply that English teachers cannot or should not take the initiative. It is only to say that the solid support and active interest of the principal and school administration are of fundamental importance. So, for a certainty, is the full participation of teachers of subjects other than English. Agreement may not be quickly reached, and probably should not be, because concrete and usable aims can be defined only through the kind of give-and-take discussion that results in genuine understanding.

Before they begin, those who are to give and take may profitably read *The Elements of Style* by Strunk and White (Macmillan, 1972). In its clarity and economy, it embodies the principles of composition it expounds. Jacques Barzun's *Simple and Direct: A Rhetoric for Writers* (Harper & Row, 1975) would also be good homework for builders of writing programs. Discussion should begin with a consideration of general aims. What do students really need to learn? Is it enough to help them gain survival skills that will spare them the handicap and embarrassment of being illiterate? If that is not enough, what more? What kind of writing, and how much, do they need to meet the demands of real life or of college work? What about creative writing? expository writing? haiku? Discussion should become increasingly specific, moving from more general aims to definite objectives (for example, paragraph control, lab reports, term papers, business letters).

When aims and objectives have been hammered out, questions of responsibility must be faced squarely—and answered clearly. How can departments other than English participate? Practically, what can teachers of science or mathematics, history or foreign language, art or music, typing or shop contribute? Can extracurricular activities play a part? What can the school administration do but smile on the program (or frown, if results fall short of hopes and expectations)? Will the principal pledge support by providing teachers time to meet for discussion of their problems and priorities? Will the principal pledge a dependable effort to keep the size of classes within reasonable limits?

Such questions must be raised, and none left without clear and definite answer if people are earnest about building a program that will foster proficiency in writing. A school has to decide what minimum level of achievement to accept. Any sensible attempt to set standards must proceed from acceptance of where, in reality, students *are* when they begin, to where the same students *can be* by the time they have completed the school's program of writing instruction. Competency tests have merit if they are preceded by unwillingness on the school's part to accept shoddy work along the way; but when promotion or graduation depends entirely on a single shot at the target, competency testing can become a reign of terror. In this connection, minimum-competency standards mandated by states or by large school districts need pose no threat. Such standards are sure to be low. In Chappaqua, New York, according to Superintendent Bernard Haake, "the kids laugh at the tests and treat them with scorn because 'they're so easy, why bother?' " If, perchance, mandated standards represent the highest for which a school can strive, so be it. If, on the other hand, they fall short of a school's reasonable expectations of its own students, that school should be able to take the standards in stride and strive for the greatest possible achievement by students.

Program builders will probably assent readily to the principle that students need to write often. This principle must not be sacrificed if program builders find it difficult in practice to arrange for writing assignments as often as once a week. There is no getting around the need, and a good program simply has to make provision for it. Mere output, of course, is not enough.

It is not the multiplication of writing assignments that counts, but motivation, selective criticism, discussion, practical explanation, and revision. Students need not only to write often, but also to write at different lengths on a variety of subjects. One research paper a term does not afford the same quality of training as a progression, for example, from a one-paragraph definition of a slang term, to a one-page composition on types of pitches used in baseball, to a two-page analysis of a simple poem, to a five-page research or process-analysis paper. It is accurate to say that the more students write, the better writers they become. And it is beneficial to point out that the example above can be followed in classes in history, science, art, music and foreign language, as well as in English classes.

Planning a proper school program takes time—and overtime—but there comes a point at which discussion has served its purpose and planners must stop talking and make a commitment. When educators reach this point, they usually draw up a long statement, turgid with jargon, that will impress the impressionable and overcome all but the still, small voices that count for little in making school decisions. Planners of writing programs must not be allowed to get away with that. They must write simply and directly; they must make a convincing case. And their plans, needless to say, must be intelligible enough for others to follow. Writing up the plan for a writing program is excellent in-service training!

In-Service Teacher Training

Something must be done to help teachers gain the assurance they need. It is not enough for them to be certified to teach; they must also be competent to teach writing. The powers that be have not yet moved to make such competence a requirement of certification in any of the states. The heat has not risen so high, and perhaps that is just as well. There is still much to learn about this particular competence, and bureaucratic attempts to define it would probably be disastrous now. Nor have the schools and departments of education risen up with one accord to be a very present help in trouble. The total neglect of writing by one college is not the whole story; new courses in teaching writing are being offered for education majors here and there. But there are no well-developed (or even developing) plans to make preparation for the teaching of writing a basic part of the preservice training of teachers. Reading, yes; writing, not yet.

It goes without saying that good preservice training would improve the general quality of the teaching of writing. At the same time, there are two reasons why in-service training—the training of teachers who are already on the job—is peculiarly important. One is the clear prospect that with declining school enrollments there will be fewer openings in the ranks of teachers. Even if we could count on teacher education to graduate whole brigades of well-trained troops, there would not be many billets for them for several years to come. We shall have to depend on teachers who are already in service—and who have not been trained—to teach writing in the schools. The second reason will obtain whether enrollments increase, decrease, or remain stable. Most of what teachers really know about teaching they learn through experience. It is the sophistication gained by experience that enables them to distinguish between sound and crackpot ideas, to follow good suggestions and reject poor ones.

In-service training is every bit as necessary as preservice preparation, but as a function of "the system" it has yet to meet the needs of teachers. Teachers seldom speak of in-service activity with interest or enthusiasm, and it is not difficult to imagine that they put in their time to satisfy somebody's mandate or perhaps to make points (any kind of points) to pull themselves up the salary scale. Good programs do exist, however, and as others take inspiration from them, in-service will probably prove to be the best way to give teachers of writing the knowledge and assurance they need. The existence of a number of in-service writing activities and the prospect of more bear witness to the probability. The arrangement that Greeley School teachers have with Robert Gundlach in Winnetka (p. 90) is just about optimum. It is an informal working arrangement in which college professor and schoolteachers help each other.

The Bay Area Writing Project is exemplary: It's not perfect, but in conception, design, and execution the project has set an example of what can and must be done if teachers are to become effective and self-assured in the teaching of writing. Beginning in 1974 with twenty-five San Francisco Bay Area teachers who were invited to take part in a five-week summer institute, the project has been extended to reach more than three thousand teachers in all quarters of the country.

This grand design grew out of the conversations of a few educators in and near San Francisco who in 1971 expressed concern about the decline of writing skills in California schools. The group included representatives from the elementary grades through graduate school. Chief among them was James Gray, then supervisor of English education at the University of California at Berkeley. From the outset, these people agreed that most teachers did not know how to teach writing because they had not been trained to write, and they acknowledged the need for continuous in-service programs that would involve both universities and school districts. One of the assumptions guiding the group's thinking was that "curriculum change cannot be accomplished by transient consultants who briefly appear, never to be seen again, or by change agents who insist that everyone see the problem in the same way."[12] When he was initiating one of the summer institutes that have been the heart of the Bay Area project, Project Director Gray told a group of teachers this:

> The BAWP philosophy runs counter to the idea of curriculum reform from the top down. It was believed for a time that we should gather together the experts in a field, find the answers—the best content and methods of instruction for that field—and then give it to teachers. . . . We don't believe this is the best way to improve instruction. Many English teachers who "know how" are successful because they believe in what they are doing, although they are all doing different things. No one method we could isolate should ever become a national curriculum for English. It's not *what* you do that makes the difference: It's the passion arising out of experience and conviction. . . . So instead of our bringing you together to give you the word, *you* are the faculty at this institute. You will teach what you do well. We'll pool information, letting ideas float to the top. You'll take back what you hear to schools who can try out these ideas.[13]

It is probably significant that Mr. Gray began his own teaching career in a high school classroom and that many of his closest associates in the project are men and women taken not from the ranks of college professors but from those of practicing schoolteachers.

This is not to suggest that the contributions of scholars and researchers are neglected by the project. On the contrary, a second basic assumption is that "a substantial body of knowledge exists concerning the teaching of writing, much of it fairly new."[14] At the same time, Mr. Gray and his associates have been realistic in the face of the fact that the distance between researchers and classroom teachers in the schools is scarcely negotiable. "No matter how solid and useful a study is," a convention of the American Educational Research Association was told not long ago, "schools are not going to buy it if a researcher is condescending, inaccessible, and unresponsive to their needs."[15] The Bay Area project is trying to negotiate the distance both by involving researchers in the project's activity and by involving participating teachers in research. The project's assumption that field-based research can make a significant contribution to the improvement of instruction is plausible, and at least, the effort will bring schoolteachers and researchers together in a novel way.

The original project has reached far beyond the San Francisco Bay Area to a dozen other centers in California (constituting the California Writing Project) and to centers in twenty or more other states. However, the pebble in the center of the ripples remains the summer invitational program on the campus of the University of California at Berkeley. This is the only program in the project that Mr. Gray conducts himself, and it is a proving ground for ideas that readily find places in the project's other centers.

The 1977 summer contingent at Berkeley was probably typical. Of twenty-six California teachers participating, one was a high school mathematics teacher and one a high school history teacher. The others were all English (or language arts) teachers: thirteen from high schools, three from junior highs, three from elementary schools, and five from colleges. There were, in addition, two high school teachers from out of state and two participating observers. In the view of the director, the primary value of the summer institutes is to develop teacher consultants who will, in turn, carry on in-service programs in the school districts. Gray tries to identify promising candidates for this role when he invites teachers to participate, and teachers who accept his invitation must be willing to serve as teacher consultants after the institute.

During their five weeks as participants, these teachers work hard. Each is responsible for a presentation on some aspect of the teaching of composition—anything from a single successful assignment to an entire curriculum sequence or a method of evaluating writing. Since they require participants to identify and describe their own best insights, the presentations often introduce new ideas to the group. At the same time they help the project director spot promising teacher consultants. Two afternoons a week are given over to visiting speakers—"outside experts" or graduates of previous summer institutes who have been leading in-service programs in school districts or serving as consultants to new centers in the project.

Perhaps the most important activity of the institute is the actual writing (and rewriting) required of each participant. Everyone is given the goal of producing four pieces of writing over the five weeks. Two afternoons a week are devoted to workshops where these grown-up teachers read their own writing to each other for comment and criticism. What begins as a very risky exposure for most of them usually proves to be a tremendously instructive experience for all. About the actual writing, Catherine Keech says,

> Writing for these groups, on our own time, introduced us all, as nothing else could, to the "process of writing" itself. Almost everyone made some discoveries about the agonies of writing to a deadline, the numb dread of exposing your work to an audience, the resistance to re-writing some things even in the face of unanimous judges, the pleasant shock of accidentally inspiring spontaneous laughter, the long, weary struggle to figure out what's really wrong with a passage, the lingering indecision after finally settling on a word that might not be exactly what we want. Teachers experienced not only what their students are likely to feel, but what they *want* their students to begin to feel as writers.[16]

Teacher consultants from the Bay Area have conducted in-service programs in sixty-five local school districts. Open to all teachers in a district, these in-service programs enroll thirty on an average, and teachers who attend are eligible for university credit. A program consists of ten or more sessions after school or on Saturday mornings, and each three-hour session features a presentation on a key issue in the teaching of composition. Through these programs and through others led by teacher consultants out of the spin-off projects (the California Writing Project and the National Writing Project), the Bay Area project has already touched as many as four hundred and fifty thousand students since the first institute was held at Berkeley in the summer of 1974.

To evaluate the project's influence on student writing and the teaching of writing, the Carnegie Corporation has funded an elaborate three-year study under the direction of Michael Scriven. The Carnegie study, in all its thirteen parts, is scheduled for completion at about the time this book goes to press. Preliminary results indicate that teachers, almost unanimously, have found the various campus and school components of the program to be extremely valuable. The design *is* a grand one, and there is an almost evangelical spirit about the project. An educational writer for the *Los Angeles Times* quotes Gray as saying, "Personally, I don't give much of a goddam about the sources and (evaluation) results. I know the project is worthwhile."[17]

The Fabric of Learning in College

Although they may not cotton to the idea, college professors must take a vital part in improving the condition of writing. Their familiar posture has been that it is up to the schools to teach students to write. "You teach 'em to read and write," a cub college instructor once said to a schoolteacher friend. "We'll educate 'em."

There is at most only a half-truth in that point of view. When matriculating freshmen happen already to be competent writers, they have still to learn how to write in and for the disciplines of higher education. Who will teach them if not the professors of those disciplines? Even more basic is the consideration that college graduates who go on to conduct the business and professional work of the country (and to teach the country's children) need to develop both their skill in writing and their understanding of the uses of writing in living and working (and in teaching). They will gain skill and understanding only to the extent that writing is part of the very fabric of their learning in college.

Since the "great American writing crisis" was declared, higher education has clicked its heels and come to attention. Crash programs and clinics are the order of the day, and no self-respecting college is without one or the other, or both. Our commission's files are stuffed with alumni magazine articles, clippings, reports, and correspondence describing (and extolling the virtues of) resurrected bonehead English classes, writing centers, laboratories, clinics, and what-have-you. In general, these activities are intended to serve two rather different purposes: *to compensate* for the deficiencies with which students come to college (and by compensating, to relieve the professoriat of the necessity), and *to help* students cope with their writing assignments. The difference is between forced feeding (bonehead classes) and voluntary nourishment (clinics and writing centers). The help motif is to be found in much of the alumni magazine literature on the subject. The writing center staff at Harvard, for example, "discourages involuntary referrals and is anxious to preserve the center as a confidential place where . . . students can work at their own pace in a nonthreatening, supportive envionment."[18] That statement reflects more than the aversion teachers now have to correcting students. The stress college writing centers place on making their services "nonthreatening" and "supportive" reflects the consequences of the frightfully unsophisticated approach to writing taken for years by many educators. The colleges, like the schools, have given students neither the time nor the support they need to learn to write well; they have given little but assignments and grades.

If the crash programs and clinics do nothing more than give students better feelings about writing, they will have rendered important service. But we think such programs will do more than that. If they succeed in giving students the kind of support that fosters confidence and stimulates interest, they will have brought about promising change. We take hope from a conversation with Cecile Hanley, who directs the writing program at Trenton State College. She told us that professors, seeing the prospect that students actually will be able to write better, are again willing to consider using essay questions on examinations. That will be the day!

But it may not be the same day that writing becomes part of the whole fabric of learning in college. Before the latter day arrives, college teachers must perceive clearly that writing is not merely a medium for testing or examining students (communication), but one of the best means students have for thinking, studying, and learning.

The perception that writing is a means of thinking, studying, and learning is probably as old as writing itself. If education has lost or neglected such a notion of writing in recent years, there have been voices in the wilderness reminding us of it—for example, the young history teacher mentioned earlier who found that his students were not just learning to write, but writing to learn. And, as we noted, Barry Beyer pointed out that writing is not an end in itself, but a learning activity. Phyllis Zagano of the State University of New York has said, "Putting language to paper is the way we make our thoughts coherent and persuasive, the principal method we use to organize the billion bits of knowledge which fill our brains."[19] And Carlos Baker of Princeton has long maintained that "learning to write is learning to think and vice versa, and I believe this is true not only in terms of the organization of one's ideas in a reasonably logical order, but also in terms of seizing the right words and putting them in the right places for clear and vigorous statement."[20]

A. D. Van Nostrand, chairman of the English Department at Brown University, has developed the idea that writing is a learning process, and through the Center for Research in Writing he has given the idea form in a program of "functional writing." Van Nostrand points out that most writing assignments "rest on the assumption that the purpose of writing is to tell someone else what you already know, with an emphasis on how much you know." His proposition inverts the usual priorities, and his program assumes that one of the important purposes of writing is to gain knowledge. "No matter how much you know about a subject, you will learn more about it by writing."[21] One of the aims of the Center for Research in Writing is to show teachers how to make writing an integral part of teaching and learning. In 1976 the center held the first of a series of seminars for Brown faculty members and undergraduates. The faculty members—a dozen of them—had been trained in the center's methods, and each undertook to present them to a group of ten students. One group was led by a teacher of Chinese; other leaders came from the classics, history, biomedicine, English, linguistics, sociology, German, and Slavic languages. Those professors believed. The center has continued the seminars at Brown, and gone on to conduct or plan them on other college campuses.

At Beaver College in Glenside, Pennsylvania, Elaine Maimon is directing a project that augurs well to prove her contention that "writing can be taught in every course and can be used to learn every course, if instructors understand that good teaching involves more than 'covering' material in lectures." Faculty members in all departments at Beaver College are working together to make "writing across the curriculum" a reality. In workshops and summer seminars they are being trained in methods of teaching writing skills, and during the academic year they work in teams to strengthen writing by planning "course clusters." A cluster involves different professors and the courses they teach, but no one's course is supplanted or abridged (there is no violation of academic freedom or integrity). The professors find a theme that will serve the purposes of each and give their students writing assignments on the theme. And they "don't just give a paper and keep talking"; they discuss the assignments with students ("prewriting") and take them through drafting and editing stages to make sure that writing serves the ends of teaching and learning. The first courses to be clustered (in the 1978 spring term) were European History since·1815, The British Literary Tradition since 1800, and Human Evolution. This is what happened:

> Students in all three courses are reading Darwin's *On the Origin of Species.* The history professor is exploring the influence of this work on the history of European thought; the English professor is examining its influence on the British literary tradition; and the biology professor is examining its influence on evolutionary theory. The faculty member in English serves as a writing consultant to this team. Team members attend each other's classes and consult together on writing assignments.[22]

Maimon reports that her expectations of faculty interest and cooperation (with each other, that is—not just with her) were exceeded and that student response was enthusiastic. During the fall 1978 term another faculty team (English, history, and religion) worked together on an American studies theme, and still another (sociology, psychology/education, and English) on "Children and the Law." The project, which is supported by the National Endowment for the Humanities, has a three-year term, and when that term is up, writing across the curriculum may very well be the "learning style" at Beaver College. It is even conceivable that writing across the curriculum will become the style across the country. The idea is not new. Carleton College in Minnesota was the first institution to have a plan of writing workshops for English and non-English faculty members, and Dr. Maimon identifies eighteen others that have active programs. The fact that she has had inquiries about the Beaver project from over sixty colleges and universities (from Santa Rosa, California, to Salem, Massachusetts) indicates that there is wide interest in something more than what is so euphemistically called compensatory education.

If the Beaver College project is on the right track, so is an experimental undergraduate course for science students at Michigan State University.[23] There, following a graduate workshop in scientific writing, Jack B. Kinsinger, chairman of the chemistry department (which sponsored the workshop) and E. Fred Carlisle (an English department member who took part in the workshop) agreed that Michigan State needed a reading and writing course emphasizing science. The meeting of their two minds led to the introduction of a course that "addresses the general writing, liberal education, and special subject area needs of undergraduate majors. Planned in detail and taught by staff from Chemistry, Physics and English," it is a year-long sequence of three terms of work and study.

The purpose of the first term's work is "to develop and define a student's general writing ability."

> By the end of the term students complete as many as ten writing assignments, as well as keep a daily journal or writing workbook. The early assignments invite mainly personal and general responses—autobiographical narratives, character studies, personal essays, and exposition. During the last three or four weeks, students shift their attention to scientific autobiographies and to operations and processes—usually scientific or technical—with which they are already familiar. Students have written in detail about telescopes, derivatives, different kinds of bicycle wheels, curve balls, isomers, and chess as well as about the growth of their interest and knowledge in science.

The second term examines the motives scientists have for writing and requires students to read rather extensively (although they continue to write). Their reading is by no means limited to professional books and papers, but includes fiction, poetry, biography, philosophic and personal essays—whatever forms scientists use in writing. During the third term, the emphasis of the course is on "the writing of functional prose—clear, direct, unambiguous, effective, and fitting writing," and students write "at least one popular essay, two scientific papers, an evaluation of a poorly written published article, and two extensive revisions."

One of the major premises of the Michigan State course is that *"the way a scientist expresses himself makes a decisive difference* in the quality and acceptance of his work, in its distribution, and in its very character." Carlisle and Kinsinger were modest in their claims for the project after the first year: "Our plan is working so far, but it has yet to be tested beyond the pilot project. . . . On the whole, however, the sequence seems to have worked very well in its first year . . . most students' writing improved." An unpublished anthology of papers written by students during the first two years of the project (1975–1977) and circulated in the field gives evidence that the project continues to work well, that science undergraduates at Michigan State are writing to become scientists.

These projects are only two of a veritable welter of new activities aimed at doing something about writing on American campuses. It must be acknowledged, however, that not *all* the current activity is new. Some colleges and universities have offered (or required) respectable courses in writing and composition for years; and among veteran teachers of freshman English (a course traditionally sloughed off on low-ranking department members), some will be shown to be the unsung heroes of a battle for better writing that has been raging for a long time. One has only to follow *Freshman English News* and NCTE's *College English* to be aware of their conscientious if not always cheerful concern in the face of back-to-basics clamor. Of the new activities, however, the Beaver College and the Michigan State projects are especially commendable because they hold promise of making writing something more than a reliable means of testing students, more than a "communications skill" usable in "the real world."

Undoubtedly equally commendable programs exist elsewhere that seek to make writing what we have called the fabric of undergraduate learning—both a resource of teaching and a means by which the students gain knowledge and become educated. To canvass them all would be premature even if it were practicable to do so, for they *are* new and their worth will not be proven for years to come. And for all the enthusiasm that characterizes those leading the field, these teachers will need sharp minds and stout hearts to win and to hold the field. Although the present "crisis" has given them an advantage, they have scarcely begun to cope with the mighty resistance that always stands in the way of institutional change. If they succeed in engaging and enlisting their colleagues, the way will be open for change, and the field may be won and held.

Epilogue

After almost half a century of educational chaos we are at last facing the brute fact that the principle of economy—use the fewest means to attain your ends—works in education as well as science and metaphysics. Students *cannot* learn everything suggested either by their own unformed tastes or by the experimental whims of certain educationists. They *must* therefore limit their learning to that which will help them live fully human lives.

But living a fully human life in itself is a great deal. Human potential is not limited to the narrowly practical, to that which enables us merely to "get along." It lies too in whatever powers of thought, feelings, and expression we may possess and in the gradual identification and release of these powers through outside guidance as well as internal development. Among these basic powers, built into the very structure of our nervous system, are those enabling us to speak, to read, to write.

The mark of a civilized being is this capacity to communicate on a level above that of the lower animals. If we neglect this capacity, if we distort it or train it poorly, we are thereby surrendering a part of our potential humanity. Undoubtedly, functional illiterates can, one way or another, live out their lives. But they remain stunted, unaware, confused, frustrated, and resentful. From their ranks may be fashioned serfs or partially mechanized humans, but not citizens of a great democracy. The challenge, therefore, is not merely to our nation's pedagogical machinery. The challenge is to our fundamental conception of ourselves as free men and women.

With many (and continuing) setbacks, our Western civilization has for thirty-five hundred years been struggling—sometimes blindly, sometimes consciously—toward the goal of individual freedom. The signature of that civilization is in part the literature it has produced. But the signature has been inscribed not by great writers alone. Whenever we ordinary men, women, and children set down a sentence clearly and truly we are also inscribing the same signature.

In that faith this book has been composed.

Appendices

Appendix A

More Reading about Writing

It might be said that American consciousness of a writing crisis was raised in December 1975 when *Newsweek*, with full cover-story flare, gave us "Why Johnny Can't Write." At virtually the same moment, however, two prominent college professors were speaking boldly and clearly to the problem. Disregarding cultural or societal excuses, both J. Mitchell Morse of Temple University and A. Bartlett Giamatti of Yale pointed directly to what they believed to be the heart of the matter—the teaching of writing in the schools. Both saw beyond the merely utilitarian function of "communications skills" to the distinctively human values of literacy.

In the fall 1975 issue of the *Temple University Alumni Review*, Morse took sharp issue with the notion that students should be free to "express themselves" in "their own language":

> Their own language, before they come to college, is in most cases the language of non-readers. It lacks the words and the syntactical structures they will need in order to live in the literate world. It is not extensive enough or varied enough to form thoughts of much complexity, and they lack experience in handling more varied and sophisticated elements. Without practice in combining many words in many ways, what can they express but naivete? Until they are exposed to writing more sophisticated than that of a comic book with a fourth-grade vocabulary and fourth-grade syntax, they will remain intellectually helpless. Teachers who lead them to believe that such poverty is not poverty are deluding them.*

---

*J. Mitchell Morse, "Green Leaves and Plausible Settings," *Temple University Alumni Review* (Philadelphia, fall 1975), pp. 14–16. Reproduced by permission. Copyright © 1976 by Temple University.

And it is worth repeating and extending here Giamatti's statement in the January 1976 *Yale Alumni Magazine:*

> High school and college students have been encouraged to believe that language does not require work—that if they wait they will suddenly blossom and flower in verbal mastery; that if they transcribe what they feel about anything it will somehow turn into what they think. Clearly, to have been told all these things—and millions of schoolchildren were and are told these things—is to have been lied to. It is also to have been robbed of the only thing that everyone *does* share, the only thing that connects us each to each. Language is the medium in which the race lives, it is what we have brought from our past, and it is what has brought us from the past—our link with who we were and who we want to be.*

Since *Newsweek*, Morse, and Giamatti made their proclamations, the country has become increasingly aware of what Phyllis Zagano has called "the great American writing crisis." The press has been replete with discussion (for lack of a better word) of the matter. Newspaper editors and columnists across the land have deplored Johnny's wretched condition while academicians of different degrees and persuasions have filled magazines and professional journals with wrangling over just what constitutes "the basics." In all this activity there has been rather more heat than light, but some offerings stand out either because they do shed light on the problem or because they provide especially keen insights into the problem.

A section of *Change* magazine (November 1976) devoted to "The Decline of Literacy" serves well to intimate the problem's complexity. There, Joan Baum of City University of New York exposes the confusion and conflict among academicians ("The Politics of Back-to-Basics"); Reney Myers of Middlesex College reports an interview with two English teachers trying to put their

---

*A. Bartlett Giamatti, "The Writing Gap: Sentimentality," *Yale Alumni Magazine* (January 1976), p. 19. Reprinted from the January 1976 issue of the *Yale Alumni Magazine;* copyright © 1976 by Yale Alumni Publications, Inc.

students in touch with language; Blyden Jackson deals with alternatives for teaching minority students and makes a case against "Black English." Mario Pei of Columbia writes of "the disturbing impact of electronic media," and Donald Stewart of Kansas State University gives a historical perspective in "The Unteachable Subject."

Phyllis Zagano, David Shanahan, and W. Dean Memering are among those whose clear insights have particular value for the muddled situation. Like Morse and Giamatti, they all see beyond "communications skills" to something deeper, more vital. Phyllis Zagano's "The Great American Writing Crisis," which deals with writing as a craft, appeared in the winter 1976–1977 issue of *Search*, the magazine of the State University of New York. She suggests that "except possibly in sports, our society has lost much of its dedication to, and awe of, great workmanship." In "Why Johnny Can't Think" (*Change*, vol. 9, number 9), Shanahan appeals for understanding of communications skills "for what they really are: tools for sharpening critical perception," and urges us to acknowledge the connection between critical thought and democracy (see page 49, this volume). Distrustful of "the back-to-basics answer to the problem" as simple-minded, Memering nevertheless acknowledges that student writing is in trouble. He comes close to the heart of the writing matter in "Forward to the Basics" (*College English*, January 1978). He would not "drag out all the old workbooks for crash courses in bonehead English," but he would "retrieve the sentence as a unit of composition from the dusty pages in the back of the handbooks and elevate it to the importance it held in classical time. . . . The sentence is a literary and rhetorical unit as well as a linguistic one; the *art* of the sentence, the *power* of the sentence are also our proper concern."

"Hard data" about student writing ability are not easily come by. Or perhaps one should say that some data are harder than others, and that no data are very hard. College Board SAT verbal scores are no measure of how well or poorly students write, of course, and the College Board tests that do provide some measure of writing ability (Test of Written English and English Composition Test) measure only the ability of some of the students who are going to some colleges—not a very meaningful sample. State and local competence tests reveal little or nothing about writing ability and serve only to reveal functional illiterates. Probably the most reliable data about Johnny's writing—if Johnny represents the average or typical American student—are the results of the National Assessment of Educational Progress tests mentioned in Chapter 1. Information about the two NAEP writing assessments made to date (1970 and 1974) is available from the National Assessment offices, Suite 700, 1800 Lincoln Street, Denver, Colorado 80203.

Conditions vary so widely from school to school that it is also difficult to come by a reliable estimate of the actual practice of teaching and learning to write. *What's Happening to American English*, by Arn M. and Charlene Tibbetts (Charles Scribner's Sons, 1978), however, is based on recent visits by the authors to English classrooms in a wide variety of schools. This book will enlighten readers and should prevent them from making careless generalizations. *A Survey of Teaching Conditions in English, 1977* has an assortment of information and all the limitations of a statistical survey based on forms completed by department chairmen alone. A short section on the teaching of composition deals chiefly with measures of total attention to writing. The survey is available from the National Council of Teachers of English, 1111 Kenyon Road, Urbana, Illinois 61801.

Literature about the teaching of writing will soon become prolific, and it is neither within our competence nor within our purpose to recommend how-to books for classroom teachers. It is our intention only to call attention to some of the writing about the teaching of writing that has caught our fancy and that we think may be of interest and value to others, whether they are teachers or not.

Earlier in the text, we quoted Ken Donelson as saying, "Any English teacher who teaches writing but who does not write is an intellectual and pedagogical fraud." The article from which that quotation was taken—"Some Responsibilities for English Teachers Who Already Face an Impossible Job" (*English Journal*, September 1977)—is a real rally. Donelson, now a professor at Arizona State University, says he has "spent twenty-five years as an English teacher, the first thirteen in Iowa high schools, the last twelve working with young people who want to be English teachers." And he lays it on the line with authority tempered by a remarkable admixture of passion and compassion. A balanced view of the English teacher's predicament is suggested by his insistence that "we need teachers who are equally unwilling to hold on to the old or to grab on to the new." His practical advice about teaching literature, language, composition, and the rest of the English teacher's portfolio is imaginative as well as forceful— for example, "We need teachers eager and able to read material aloud that just might interest, intrigue, amuse, or excite the kids, material which might sometimes intend to make young people aware of new or old books or writers or techniques or ideas." Donelson concludes that "it's a frustrating and tiring life, but it's a life we must live if we care about literature, language, writing, nonprint media, education, and above all the kids we face. Why do we stay in this impossible job? Simple answer—because we're English teachers and that's what our racket consists of. There isn't any other answer."

Balance the Basics: Let Them Write is a 1978 report to the Ford Foundation by Donald H. Graves of the University of New Hampshire. Based on firsthand knowledge of teaching and learning in many schools, the report begins with this statement of the fundamental importance of writing:

> People want to write. The desire to express is relentless. People want others to know what they hold to be truthful. They need the sense of authority that goes with authorship. They need to detach themselves from experience and examine it by writing. Then they need to share what they have discovered through writing.

Noting that "for every dollar spent on teaching writing a hundred or more are spent on teaching reading," Graves pays strict attention to practices in the schools when he answers the question, "Why don't we write?" He bemoans the fact that "orders for lined paper, principally used for writing composition, are going down," but he is confident that "barriers to good writing are not as high or insurmountable as they seem. . . . Good teaching *does* produce good writing. There *are* schools where writing and expression are valued." In the third and final section of the thirty-two page report, Graves comes conscientiously to grips with how writing can be taught, describing in detail "a proven, workable way to reverse the decline of writing in our schools." The report is available from the Ford Foundation, 320 East Forty-Third Street, New York, New York 10017.

Although her title is formidably straightforward, Janet Emig's *The Composing Process of Twelfth Graders* is—as a foreword advertises—lucid, provocative, "and at times disconcertingly outspoken." It is also interesting and instructive. The word *process* has come into vogue to distinguish the intellectual effort that writing is from the mechanical procedure it is commonly presumed to be. This study looks right into the process. Adapting the now familiar case-study method to her own purpose, Emig investigates the minds of eight students from different backgrounds and different secondary schools to find out what actually happens when they are writing. What she finds prompts her to call the conventional five-paragraph theme an "essentially redundant form, devoid, or duplicating, of content in at least two of its five parts." She concludes that there is little correlation between what is being taught students in school and the practices of the best current writers, and she suggests candidly that this "absence of match . . . is partially attributable to teacher illiteracy." Even more crucial, Emig contends, is the fact that "many teachers of composition, at least below the college level, themselves do not write" and accordingly "err in important ways. They underconceptualize and oversimplify the process of composing. Planning degenerates into outlining; reformulating becomes the correction of minor infelicities." She is bold to say that "much of the teaching of composition in American high schools is essentially a neurotic activity." Stressing the point that writing in schools tends to be "other-directed" and "other-centered," and that "too often, the other is a teacher," Emig is persuaded that "the most significant others in the . . . writing of twelfth graders are peers, despite the overwhelming opportunity for domination teachers hold." This conclusion leads her to a final assertion:

American high schools and colleges must seriously and immediately consider that the teacher-centered presentation of composition, like the teacher-centered presentation of almost every other segment of a curriculum, is pedagogically, developmentally, and politically an anachronism.

Not everyone will need or want to read the entire study from page one to page one hundred (and fifty more pages of appendices and bibliography), but browsing the case studies (Chapters 4 and 5) and close reading of the findings (Chapter 6) and the implications (Chapter 7) should be required of everyone who cares about the teaching of writing. The report is available from the National Council of Teachers of English, 1111 Kenyon Road, Urbana, Illinois 61801.

It is difficult to distinguish between the virtues and the values of Mina Shaughnessy's *Errors and Expectations* (Oxford University Press, 1977). Free of pedagogical jargon, the book treats its difficult subject with engaging style and imagination and clearly reflects the quality of a teacher who cares as much for her students as she does for her discipline. *Errors and Expectations* is drawn from Shaughnessy's experience with the first waves of open admissions freshmen at the City University of New York. Many of those students were "academic losers," whose writing was "stunningly unskilled" and whose problems were apparently "irremediable." But such students are America's Johnnys, and New York has no monopoly. There are more in some schools than in others, to be sure, but across the country in rural, suburban, and urban schools are students for whom "academic writing is a trap"; for whom "writing is but a line which moves haltingly across the page, exposing as it goes all that the writer doesn't know, then passing into the hands of a stranger who reads it with a lawyer's eyes, searching for flaws."

Professor Shaughnessy's book is a guide for Johnnys' teachers—not, she carefully points out, a program, but a guide. She divides the "territory of difficulty" into familiar teaching categories that serve as headings for the main sections of the book: Handwriting and Punctuation, Syntax, Common Errors, Spelling, Vocabulary, and Beyond the Sentence. The book is not easy going and may require more than one rereading. But most readers will find it interesting, while teachers are likely to find that they are "carrying many things they will not be needing, that will clog their journey" into the territory of difficulty. "So too they will discover the need of other things they do not have and will need to fabricate by mother wit out of whatever is at hand." The book's wealth of wisdom and common sense is anticipated in a concluding paragraph of the introduction:

But when we move out of the centuries and into Monday morning, into the life of the young man or woman sitting in a basic writing class, our linguistic contemplations are likely to hover over a more immediate reality—namely, the fact that a person who does not control the dominant code of literacy in a society that generates more writing than any society in history is likely to be pitched against more obstacles than are apparent to those who have already mastered that code. From such a vantage point, one feels the deep conserving pull of language, the force that has preserved variant dialects of English as well as the general dialect of literacy, and one knows that errors matter, knows further that a teacher who would work with basic writing students might well begin by trying to understand the logic of their mistakes in order to determine at what point or points along the developmental path error should or can become a subject for instruction. What I hope will emerge from this exploration into error is not a new way of sectioning off students' problems with writing but rather a readiness to look at these problems in a way that does not ignore the linguistic sophistication of the students nor yet underestimate the complexity of the task they face as they set about learning to write for college.*

Scholarly research of "the cognitive and linguistic process" we call writing has to provide us with more of practical value than such research has to date. The field has not been cultivated systematically, nor has the fruit of research often been retailed with wide appeal. The complaint that researchers write only for each other is not without some justification. Nevertheless, the good work that has been done should not be overlooked or neglected.

From "a substantial body of knowledge concerning the teaching of writing, much of it fairly new" James Gray and Miles Myers of the Bay Area Writing Project single out the work of Francis Christensen (*Notes Toward a New Rhetoric*, Harper & Row, 1968), Josephine Miles ("What We Compose," National

---

*Mina Shaughnessy, *Errors and Expectations* (New York: Oxford University Press, 1977), p. 13. Reproduced by permission. Copyright © 1977 by Oxford University Press. Other statements by Shaughnessy are from her Introduction, pp. 1-13.

Council of Teachers of English, 1963; "Essay in Reason," *Educa-tional Leader*, 1958; *Style and Proportion: The Language of Prose and Poetry*, Little, Brown, 1967), and James Moffett (*Teaching the Universe of Discourse* and *A Student-Centered Language Arts Curriculum, K–13*, Houghton-Mifflin, 1968).

Readers who want to browse the field might refer to *Help for the Teacher of Written Composition: New Directions in Research.* Edited by Sara W. Lundsteen, this seventy-two-page ERIC/NCRE bulletin offers "a brief historical overview of the teaching and inquiry that have occurred in this country and a discussion of the last few decades of serious investigation in the area of written composition at the elementary level." Those in-terested in the teaching of composition in high school may find Rodney Barth's annotated bibliography (*English Journal*, January 1977) suggestive. Richard L. Larsen's "Selected Bibliography of Research and Writing about the Teaching of Composition, 1977" (*College Composition and Communication*, May 1978) appears to be more extensive and comprehensive. All these publications are available from the National Council of Teachers of English, 1111 Kenyon Road, Urbana, Illinois 61801.

In the summer of 1977 the National Institute of Education brought some fifty scholars, teachers, and other professional peo-ple together for a conference on "the nature, development, and teaching of writing." Never before had there been such an assemblage. Anthropologists, linguists, psychologists, semanti-cists, teachers of writing, teachers of literature—these were experts all, who, in many instances, were unfamiliar with the concerns and work of the others. In addition, business and professional people were present who were concerned about the condition of American writing. The conference was a kind of show-and-tell affair. Each participant presented a paper reflecting his work (or worry), and the discussion that followed in every case was calcu-lated to identify the questions about writing that really need to be raised.

That NIE conference may have helped to bring research to an important watershed.* More of the right questions about writing

*Some of the conference papers are being edited and compiled for publication under the title, *Writing: The Nature, Development and Teaching of Written Composition.* Carl H. Fredericksen, Marcia Farr Whiteman, and Joseph F. Dominic are the editors.

are being asked now. And if the scholars who look for the answers—those people who write about writing—put their findings in writing that has some style and imagination, then teachers and students of writing will be able to count on research for help that is at once significant and substantial.

We add two short, well-known books of more general interest, referred to in the text but well worth the extra emphasis. These books probably ought to be on the shelves of all English teachers and indeed all those who have even a frail connection with the business of writing. The first is *The Elements of Style*, the little handbook by William Strunk, Jr. It was revived to new fame by E. B. White, who in this new paperback edition (Macmillan, 1972) supplies some revisions and adds a charming introduction plus a chapter on writing. The second title is *Simple and Direct: A Rhetoric for Writers*, by Jacques Barzun (Harper & Row, 1975). It has already quietly established itself as a minor classic in its field.

James Howard

Appendix B

Readaloudables for Children from Three to Seven

Writing begins long before the marriage of pencil and paper. It begins with sounds, that is to say with words and simple clusters of words that are taken in by small children until they find themselves living in a world of vocables. If that world is rich and exciting, the transition to handling it in a new medium—writing—is made smoother. The first and conceivably the most important instructor in composition is the teacher, parent, or older sibling who reads aloud to the small child. That is why this list of books is quite properly part of a book on the teaching and learning of writing. Indeed, it may be by far the most useful part.

There are many lists as good or better, many much longer, many more comprehensive. In compiling this one I have had certain requirements in mind. I have tried to think of the "average" child from three to seven, neither highly sensitive nor backward. I have paid no attention to ethnic representation, preferring to think of the child merely as a child and not as a member of an oppressed or favored minority. Nor is any of these books tendentious. I do not believe the aim of reading aloud is to turn the little listeners into world citizens, revolutionaries, idealists, patriots, Zoroastrians. The aim is to fill them with interesting language and make them feel the delight of words placed in an effective order.

I admit also that this is a conservative list. Dozens, perhaps hundreds, of more recent books are as good as these. But I have preferred to accept the judgment of time: if a book for children has lived for a decade or more, it must have something. I've kept two other criteria in mind as well. First, the book must really sound good when read aloud—not all children's books, even the finest, satisfy this requirement. Second, I have included no book that has not given me, an old man, pleasure.

156

So do not scold me for leaving out your favorites or for including some that may not have worked in your family or classroom. This is a personal list that satisfies the criteria above mentioned, no more than that. It is really intended for parents (and perhaps even some teachers) who *have* no favorites, who do not know where to begin, and who are confused by the bright chaos of children's literature.

Children's books are far more expensive than they should be. Wherever possible I have suggested paperback editions and have so indicated. But new paperback editions constantly appear; consult your bookseller.

Nursery Rhymes

Nursery rhymes are the place to begin, of course. It is a happy fact that the conventional first item of children's literature, Mother Goose, is also one of the greatest, and far and away the best for reading aloud. When I say "best" I mean, among other bests, best for instructional purposes. Mother Goose's language is vigorous, vivid, funny, and economical. It has an advantage for our time that did not exist a century ago. Its vocabulary is just a little out-of-date, but in a good sense. For example, if you read aloud the most famous of all the rhymes, "Jack and Jill," your child will, after listening to the third line, have learned the excellent word *fetch*. This word has a useful, precise meaning, a little different from *get*. It should not be allowed to disappear. Mother Goose will see to that.

I suggest having available two different editions. The first should be a beautifully illustrated one, to catch small children's eyes and make them see at once that the rhymes are about perfectly solid, material people and things. There are dozens of lovely Mother Gooses. A good one is *The Tall Book of Mother Goose*, illustrated by Feodor Rojankovsky (Harper & Row). But you also need a *complete* Mother Goose furnishing hours of reading aloud, one not particularly designed to be looked at, though it will usually contain some black-and-white illustrations. Recommended are Iona and Peter Opie, *Oxford Nursery Rhyme Book* (Oxford, paperback) or Iona and Peter Opie, *Puffin Book of Nursery Rhymes* (Penguin, paperback).

Verse

Keep in mind that children have to be taught to dislike verse. Rhyme, rhythm, cadence, imagery, cunningly contrived sound— all are natural, indeed irresistible, to them when young. The best book of verse for small children ever compiled is Mother Goose. But you'll need, for variety, a good anthology. Again, hundreds exist. I like (but it goes beyond age seven) Nancy Larrick, *Piping Down the Valleys Wild* (Dell, paperback) and also James Reeves, *The Merry-Go-Round* (Penguin, paperback). For very small children try Leslie Brooke, *Johnny Crow's Garden* (Watts, paperback), though the rhyme here is incidental to the story. The best living writer of children's verse (one man's opinion) is David Mc-Cord, some of whose work is probably for older children. He has collected himself in *One at a Time* (Little, Brown). Among the classics the best for reading aloud is Edward Lear, *Complete Nonsense* (Dover, paperback). Two other first-rate books of children's verse, quite different in appeal, are Clyde Watson, *Father Fox's Pennyrhymes* (Scholastic Book Service, paperback) and Elizabeth Madox Roberts, *Under the Tree* (Viking). The latter is for children destined to be latter-day Keatses. Finally, though A. A. Milne may seem a little odd to the child already rotted by television (I don't think he will), there are his *When We Were Very Young* (Dell, paperback) and *Now We Are Six* (Dell, paperback). Post-finally, I recommend any of Dr. Seuss's immense library of verse narratives but especially *And to Think That I Saw It on Mulberry Street* (Hale).

Traditional Folk and Fairy Tales

Most small children like folk and fairy tales. Not all do. Hundreds of collections are available. I will suggest only two: *Tales from Grimm* and *More Tales from Grimm*, written and illustrated by Wanda Gág (Coward).

Stories and Sort-of-Stories

Stories, of course, are the mainstay. For three to seven's they should not be too long, they should if possible be funny, they should be reassuring, a lot of them should be about animals, and the pictures should attract. Beyond this, they should not have been tailored to meet the market demands but be the work of genuine writers and artists. I list a few titles, again warning you that there are perhaps several hundred others almost as good, and perhaps better (though I don't *think* so). All old favorites. They are arranged, very roughly, in order of increasing difficulty.

• Dorothy Kunhardt, *Pat the Bunny* (Western Publishing) comes with a little bunny-gadget the children can pat. Never fails.

• Margaret Wise Brown, *The Little Fireman* (Scholastic Book Service, paperback), *Goodnight Moon* (Harper & Row, paperback), and indeed any of her more than twenty titles.

• Beatrix Potter, any of her twenty-four titles, all published by Warne, but perhaps especially *The Tale of Peter Rabbit*, *The Tale of Benjamin Bunny*, *The Tale of Tom Kitten*, *The Tale of Mrs. Tiggy-winkle*. Miss (she would scorn Ms.) Potter is to the tale for teenies what Tolstoy is to the novel.

• Wanda Gág, *Millions of Cats*, *The Funny Thing*, *Snippy and Snappy* (all Coward).

• Marie Hall Ets, *Play with Me*, *In the Forest* (Viking, both paperback).

• Ruth Krauss, *I'll Be You—You Be Me* (Bookstore Press, paperback). *A Hole Is to Dig* (Harper & Row). Lovely nonsense, with great Sendak illustrations.

• Virginia Lee Burton, *The Little House* and *Mike Mulligan and His Steam Shovel* (Houghton Mifflin).

• Else Homelund Minarik, any of her titles but especially *Little Bear* and *A Kiss for Little Bear* (both Harper & Row).

• Hardie Gramatky, *Little Toot* and *Little Toot on the Grand Canal* (both Putnam).

• Leo Lionni, *Frederick* and *Swimmy* (Pantheon, both paperbacks). Marvelous art work.

• Arnold Lobel, any of his titles, especially *Mouse Tales* (paperback) and *Frog and Toad Are Friends* (both Harper & Row).

• Jean de Brunhoff (make sure it's Jean, not Laurent), any of the Babar books, especially *The Story of Babar, Babar the King, Babar and His Children* (all Random House).

• Robert McCloskey, *Make Way for Ducklings, Homer Price* (both Viking, both paperback).

• Ezra Jack Keats, *Hi Cat!* (Macmillan, paperback), *The Snowy Day* (Viking, paperback), *Whistle for Willie* (Viking, paperback).

• Astrid Lindgren, *The Tomten* (Coward). A superb rendering of a Swedish folktale.

• Robert Lawson, *Rabbit Hill* (Dell, paperback).

• H. A. Rey, *Curious George* (Houghton Mifflin, paperback).

• Louise Fatio, *The Happy Lion* (McGraw-Hill).

• Munro Leaf, *The Story of Ferdinand* (Viking, paperback).

• Albert Lamorisse, *The Red Balloon* (Doubleday); one of the few children's stories using real-life photographs successfully.

That's a little over fifty titles, a good start on a library of read-aloudables for children who cannot yet write or are just beginning to learn.

Clifton Fadiman

Notes

Introduction
1. Jacques Barzun, "The State of Writing Today" (Unpublished speech given at the University of Texas at Arlington, 3 March 1977).
2. Arn Tibbetts and Charlene Tibbetts, *What's Happening to American English?* (New York: Charles Scribner's Sons, 1978), p. 100.
3. Information on the British situation and the quote from the Plowden Report are from C. B. Cox and Rhodes Boyson, eds., *Black Paper* (London: Temple Smith, 1977), pp. 5–7.

Chapter 1
1. *New York Times*, 4 May 1978.
2. *Newsweek*, 8 December 1975, p. 59.
3. *The Valley Voice* (Middlebury, Vt.), 14 December 1977.
4. Robert H. McBride, "Industry's View of Recent High School Graduates—Five Interviews," from "Minimum Graduation Standards," assembled and edited by Robert H. McBride, National Association of State Boards of Education, Denver, Colo.
5. James J. Kilpatrick, *San Francisco Chronicle*, 1 November 1977.
6. Material on the NAEP findings comes from the National Assessment of Educational Progress's *Writing Mechanics, 1969–1974* (Washington, D.C.: U.S. Government Printing Office, 1975; report 05-W-01).
7. Comments by Richard Lloyd-Jones, Ross Winterowd, and Roy H. Forbes on the NAEP findings were quoted in NAEP, *Writing Mechanics*.
8. Council for Basic Education *Bulletin* (February 1972 and February 1976).
9. Panel chaired by Willard Wirtz, *On Further Examination* (New York: College Entrance Examination Board, 1977).
10. "The SAT Scores Decline," Council for Basic Education *Bulletin* (October 1977).
11. Raymond English, "Back to Basics: A Chance for Educational Reform," *The University Bookman* (winter 1978), p. 34.
12. San Bernardino *Sun-Times*, 29 January 1977.
13. James D. Koerner, *The Teaching of Expository Writing* (New York: Alfred P. Sloan Foundation, 1977).

14. *Look,* 21 June 1961.
15. William B. Fretter, "Preparation for Admission to the University" (A report to the Committee on Educational Policy of the Regents of the University of California, 18 November 1976).
16. Elissa S. Guralnik and Paul M. Levitt, "Improving Student Writing: A Case History," *College English* (January 1977).
17. *New York Times,* 7 February 1977.
18. Donald C. Stewart, "A Cautionary Tale: The Unteachable Subject," in "The Decline of Literacy," a special section in *Change* (November 1976), pp. 48–51.
19. *New York Times,* 7 February 1977.
20. Joan Baum's article is also found in "Decline of Literacy," *Change* (November 1976), pp. 32–33.
21. Information about and comments on the Dartmouth situation come from Shelby Grantham's "Johnny Can't Write? Who Cares?" *Dartmouth Alumni Magazine* (January 1977).
22. Rexford Brown and Richard Lloyd-Jones are quoted in the NAEP report *Writing Mechanics.*

Chapter 2
1. Lois DeBakey, "Literacy: Mirror of Society," *Journal of Technical Writing and Communication* 8(1978):286–87. All quotes from DeBakey's "Literacy" are by permission of the publisher. Copyright © 1978 Baywood Publishing Company, Inc., Farmingdale, N.Y.
2. DeBakey, "Literacy," pp. 291–92.
3. *The Dialogues of Plato,* trans. B. Jowett (New York: Random House, 1937), p. 278.
4. Jerry Mander, *Four Arguments for the Elimination of Television* (New York: William Morrow & Co., 1978).
5. DeBakey's comments on television which follow are from "Literacy," pp. 307–12.
6. DeBakey, "Literacy," p. 281.
7. Lois DeBakey and Selma DeBakey, "Medicant," *Forum on Medicine* 1(1978):85.
8. DeBakey, "Literacy," pp. 294–95.
9. A. Bartlett Giamatti, "Why Young People Today Can't Write," *National Observer,* 17 October 1976.

Chapter 3
1. Stephen White's remarks are found in "A Response to Albert H. Bowker," in James D. Koerner, ed., *The Teaching of Expository Writing* (New York: Alfred P. Sloan Foundation, 1977).
2. National Assessment of Educational Progress, *Writing Mechanics 1969–1974* (Washington, D.C.: U.S. Government Printing Office, 1975, report 05-W-01).

3. George Weber, "Back to Basics in the Schools" (Unpublished manuscript), p. 15.
4. Jacques Barzun, "The State of Writing Today" (Unpublished speech given at the University of Texas at Arlington, 3 March 1977).
5. Unless otherwise noted, statements by Charles Scribner quoted in this chapter are from his paper written for the commission.
6. Aidan Chambers, "Talking about Reading: Back to Basics?" *Hornbook* (October 1977).
7. W. Dean Memering, "Forward to the Basics," *College English* (January 1978), pp. 554–55.
8. James Fenimore Cooper, *The American Democrat*, vol. 14, 1838.
9. Daniel Shanahan, "Why Johnny Can't Think," *Change* (September 1977), p. 10.
10. Ronald Berman, "On Writing Good," *New York Times*, 29 January 1978.
11. Courtney B. Cazden, "Language, Literacy, and Literature," *Principal* (October 1977), pp. 40–42.
12. Barzun, "The State of Writing," University of Texas speech.

Chapter 4

1. E. D. Hirsch, Jr., *The Philosophy of Composition* (Chicago: University of Chicago Press, 1977), pp. 11–23. © 1977 by The University of Chicago. All rights reserved. Published 1977.
2. Hirsch, *The Philosophy of Composition*, p. 37.
3. From Richard Braddock, Richard Lloyd-Jones, and Lowell Schoer, *Research in Written Composition* (National Council of Teachers of English, 1963), p. 37, as quoted in Charles Weingarten, "Getting to Some Basics That the Back-to-Basics Movement Doesn't Get To," *English Journal* (October 1977), p. 41.
4. Unless otherwise noted, statements by Jacques Barzun in this chapter are from his unpublished working paper written for the commission.
5. Carl Bereiter, Peter J. Gamlin, Valerie Anderson, and Marlene Scardamalia, "A General Proposal Aimed at Development of a Pedagogy of Writing" (Unpublished manuscript), pp. 16–17. Copyright © 1977 by the authors and reproduced by permission. This material has since been published, with the same title, by Open Court Publishing Co., La Salle, Ill.
6. Frank Heys, Jr., "The Theme-a-Week Assumption: Report of an Experiment," *English Journal* (May 1962), pp. 320–22, as quoted in Weingarten, "Getting to Some Basics," p. 41.
7. James Barrie, *Sentimental Tommy* (currently in print as vol. 5 of *The Works of James M. Barrie*, 18 vols., New York, AMS Press), 1975.
8. Hirsch, *The Philosophy of Composition*, p. 142.

9. A. Bartlett Giamatti, quoted in George Weber in "Back to Basics in the Schools," (Unpublished manuscript), p. 98.
10. Arn Tibbetts and Charlene Tibbetts, *What's Happening to American English* (New York: Charles Scribner's Sons, 1978), p. 73.
11. Hirsch, *The Philosophy of Composition*, p. 8.

Chapter 5

1. Don Marquis, *Archy and Mehitabel* (New York: Doubleday, 1927), p. 13.
2. Dorothy H. Cohen, "Through a Glass Darkly: Television and the Perception of Reality," *Principal* (January/February 1977), p. 24.
3. David Mackay and Joseph Simp, *Help Your Child to Read and Write, and More* (New York: Penguin Books, 1976), p. 62.
4. Donald H. Graves, *Balance the Basics: Let Them Write* (New York: Ford Foundation, 1978), p. 10.
5. Dorothy Wilson, "Competency Testing without Difficulties," Council for Basic Education *Bulletin* (October 1977), pp. 10–11.
6. This and other observations by Robert Gundlach are reproduced by permission from his unpublished paper "When Children Write; Notes for Parents and Teachers on Children's Written Language Development," copyright © 1976 by Robert A. Gundlach. The paper was prepared for distribution to the parents of children in the Winnetka Public Schools, Winnetka, Ill. Copies are available from the author c/o Department of Linguistics, Northwestern University, 2016 Sheridan Road, Evanston, Ill. 60201.
7. Helen Danforth's comments and the information on the Samuel Greeley School program were conveyed in personal communications to James Howard.
8. Carl Bereiter, Peter J. Gamlin, Valerie Anderson, and Marlene Scardamalia, "A General Proposal Aimed at Development of a Pedagogy of Writing" (Unpublished manuscript), pp. 29–30. Copyright © 1977 by the authors and reproduced by permission. This material has since been published, with the same title, by Open Court Publishing Co., La Salle, Ill.
9. W. Dean Memering, "Forward to the Basics," *College English* (January 1978), pp. 554–55.
10. Anne Obenchain, "How We Can Teach Johnny to Read and Write" (Unpublished paper), 1976.
11. An account of this class, including the stories of several students, appeared in the magazine section of the *Sunday Freeman* (Ulster County, N.Y.), 23 April 1978.
12. Obenchain, "How We Can Teach Johnny."
13. Barry Beyer, "Teaching the Basics in Social Studies," *Social Education* (February 1977).
14. *New York Times*, 7 May 1977, Op-Ed page.

Chapter 6

1. This and the following comment are in a letter from Alida Woods, Asheville, N.C., to James Howard.
2. *Claremont* (Calif.) *Courier*, October 1977.
3. Ken Donelson, "Some Responsibilities for English Teachers Who Already Face an Impossible Job," *English Journal* (September 1977), p. 30.
4. Lucy McCormick Calkins, "Children Discover What Writers Know," *Learning* (April 1978), p. 36.
5. A current source for this story, originally published in 1902, is Joseph Conrad, *Typhoon and Other Tales* (New York: New American Library, 1963).
6. Barry Beyer, "Teaching the Basics in Social Studies," *Social Education* (February 1977).
7. E. Fred Carlisle, "Teaching Scientific Writing Humanistically; From Theory To Action," *English Journal* (April 1978), p. 35.
8. Wallace W. Douglas, "Composition and the Editorial Process," *Reflections on High School English*, ed. Gary Tate, (Tulsa, Okla.: University of Tulsa, 1966), pp. 76–90.
9. Courtney B. Cazden, "Language, Literacy, and Literature," *Principal* (October 1977), pp. 40–42.
10. Carl Bereiter, Peter J. Gamlin, Valerie Anderson, and Marlene Scardamalia, "A General Proposal Aimed at Development of a Pedagogy of Writing" (Unpublished manuscript), p. 24. Copyright © 1977 by the authors and reproduced by permission. This material has since been published, with the same title, by Open Court Publishing Co., La Salle, Ill.
11. Paul Kalkstein, "Competence and Beyond: A Manual for Teachers of Writing" (Unpublished manuscript).
12. Daniel Fader, *Hooked on Books* (New York: Berkeley Publishing Corp., 1976), pp. 12–22.

Chapter 7

1. James Reston, quoted in Council for Basic Education *Bulletin* (May 1977).
2. Alfred Kahn, quoted in Council for Basic Education *Bulletin* (January 1978).
3. Charles Weingartner, "Muttering," *English Journal* (April 1978).
4. *New York Times*, 3 May 1978.
5. From a resolution adopted by the annual meeting of the National Council of Teachers of English, 1977.
6. Elaine P. Maimon, "Team Efforts to Teach Writing in All Disciplines: The Beaver College Plan," *PCTE Bulletin* (April 1978).
7. "Florida Takes a Test," Council for Basic Education *Bulletin* (February 1978).

8. Ibid.
9. Information on the Dartmouth, Mass., curriculum is available from Arthur Bennett, Dartmouth High School, Dartmouth, Mass. 02714.
10. Information concerning the Fairfax curriculum is contained in *The Guide for Teaching Writing* (for teachers of grades 7–12), published by Fairfax County Public Schools, 10700 Page Ave., Fairfax, Va. 22003. Price of the guide is $1.55; address requests to the attention of Mrs. Betty Blaisdell. A guide for teachers K–6 was scheduled for completion in fall 1979.
11. James Gray and Miles Myers, "The Bay Area Writing Project," *Phi Delta Kappan* (February 1978), p. 413.
12. Gray and Myers, "The Bay Area Writing Project," p. 411.
13. This paraphrase of Mr. Gray's remarks and much of the descriptive material about the Bay Area Writing Project comes from Catherine Keech, "The Bay Area Writing Project: A Description and Evaluation," unpublished paper written by the author in her role as an evaluating observer in the project's 1977 summer institute, held on the Berkeley campus of the University of California. Further information about the project and its affiliates in other states may be obtained by writing to the Bay Area Writing Project, Department of Education, University of California, Berkeley, Calif. 94720.
14. Gray and Myers, "The Bay Area Writing Project," p. 411.
15. *Education U.S.A.* (April 11, 1977).
16. Keech, "A Description and Evaluation."
17. *Los Angeles Times*, 6 June 1977.
18. Thea Singer, "The Writing Center: Helping People to Find Their Own Voice," *Radcliffe Quarterly* (June 1977).
19. Phyllis Zagano, "The Great American Writing Crisis," *Search* (A publication of the State University of New York, winter 1976–1977).
20. Carlos Baker's statement comes from a letter to James Howard.
21. A. D. Van Nostrand described the program's basis in a Brown University memorandum, 26 August 1976. For information about functional writing, write the Center for Research in Writing, P.O. Box 2317, Providence, R.I. 02906.
22. Information on the Beaver College program comes primarily from Elaine P. Maimon, "Team Efforts to Teach Writing in All Disciplines: The Beaver College Plan," *PCTE Bulletin* (April 1978). For current information, contact Elaine P. Maimon, Director, Writing Program, Beaver College, Glenside, Penn. 19038.
23. Information about the Michigan State University program is taken from an article by E. Fred Carlisle and Jack B. Kinsinger, "Scientific Writing," *Journal of Chemical Education* (October 1977).